ACTUARIAL CONSIDERATIONS REGARDING RISK AND RETURN IN PROPERTY-CASUALTY INSURANCE PRICING

Oakley E. Van Slyke, Editor

May, 1999

Library of Congress Card Number: 99-067615

ISBN 0-9624762-1-8

Printed for the Society by

Kirby Lithographic Company, Inc.

Arlington, Virginia

Actuarial Considerations Regarding Risk and Return in Property-Casualty Insurance Pricing

Oakley E. Van Slyke, Editor

May, 1999

ACTUARIAL CONSIDERATIONS REGARDING RISK AND RETURN IN PROPERTY-CASUALTY INSURANCE PRICING

CONTENTS

Acknowledgment

I am indebted to the members of the Valuation and Financial Analysis Committee and its Chairman, Susan Witcraft, for their support and guidance. The book would not have been possible without the dedication and patience of the authors. I am also indebted to Giuseppe Russo, Ph. D., ASA, for his careful review of the book and his reworking of the mathematical notation in several chapters to promote consistency. The opinions are those of the authors; any editorial errors or omissions are my own.

The significant contribution of the Actuarial Education and Research Fund in funding this project is gratefully acknowledged.

Oakley E. Van Slyke
San Clemente, California
March, 1998

Contributors

Russell E. Bingham is Director, Corporate Research, for the Hartford Insurance Group in Hartford, CT.

Stephen P. D'Arcy, FCAS, MAAA, Ph D, is Professor of Finance, University of Illinois at Urbana-Champaign. He currently serves on the CAS Textbook Steering Committee, on the Dynamic Financial Analysis Task Force on Variables and as the CAS's liaison to the American Risk and Insurance Association (ARIA). Steve is president-elect of ARIA. For the past four years Steve has taught a Limited Attendance Seminar on Principles of Finance for the CAS.

Robert P. Eramo, ACAS, MAAA, is President, Risk Assessment & Strategies, Inc, of New York. His papers include, "A Study of the Effects of Asset/Liability Mismatch on Property/Casualty Insurance Companies," Call Papers on Valuation Issues, 1989.

Rodney Kreps, FCAS, MAAA, Ph D, is Senior Vice President and Chief Actuary with Sedgwick Re Insurance Strategy, Inc., of Seattle. Rodney authored "Reinsurer Risk Loads from Marginal Surplus Requirements," Proceedings of the Casualty Actuarial Society, 1990. He currently serves as Vice Chairman of the Casualty Actuarial Society's Committee on the Theory of Risk.

Charles L. McClenahan, FCAS, ASA, MAAA, is a Principal with William M. Mercer, Inc., in Deerfield, IL. Chuck is the author of the chapter titled "Ratemaking" in the CAS textbook Foundations of Casualty Actuarial Science. He has published two papers on models of the loss development process in the Proceedings of the Casualty Actuarial Society and many other articles and papers. Chuck has been active in the committee work of the CAS since 1975 and served as a Director from 1979 to 1982 and from 1987 to 1989.

Judith Mintel is Associate General Counsel in the Corporate Law Department of State Farm Mutual Automobile Insurance Company. Ms. Mintel was formerly Deputy Insurance Commissioner of the Commonwealth of Virginia and currently is an Adjunct Professor of Law, University of Illinois Law School. She is the author of Insurance Rate Litigation published by Kluwer-Nijhoff.

Frank D. Pierson, FCAS, MAAA, is Managing Director of Zurich Centre ReSource Limited, New York. Frank is past chair of the CAS Joint Program Committee for Reinsurance Seminars.

Ira Robbin, Ph D, is Assistant Vice President at CIGNA Property and Casualty and heads the CIGNA Special Risk Facilities Casualty Actuarial Unit, Philadelphia. Ira is the author of the CAS's study note, "The Underwriting Profit Provision," and has taught many actuarial examination preparation seminars.

Charles F. Toney II, FCAS, MAAA, is Vice President and Chief Actuary of Mercury General Corporation, Los Angeles. Charles's principal responsibility is pricing personal lines insurance products.

Oakley E. Van Slyke, FCAS, ASA, MAAA, is President of Capital Management Technology[SM] of San Clemente, California. Lee has written more than 20 articles and papers, including "Regulatory Standards for Reserves," CAS Discussion Paper Program, 1987; "Solvency Standards," AFIR 1992; and "A General Theory of Finance," AFIR 1995. He served on the CAS's Valuation and Financial Analysis Committee and its predecessor committee from 1991 to 1997.

PREFACE

The Casualty Actuarial Society adopted the Statement of Principles Regarding Property and Casualty Ratemaking in May, 1988. That Statement of Principles states,

> The rate should include a charge for the risk of random variation from the expected costs. This risk charge should be reflected in the determination of the appropriate total return consistent with the cost of capital and, therefore, influences the underwriting profit provision. (lines 131 to 133)

In the literature of pricing, accounting profits are generally seen to result from three things: the reward for the time value of money, the reward for exposing capital to risk, and the reward for better-than-average operations. The management of an insurance company might reasonably take responsibility for the extent to which profit will be expected to arise from better-than-average operations. The actuary, however, by training and experience is equipped to assist management to understand the time value of money and the cost of exposing capital to risk.

There is a great deal of intellectual activity about the time value of money and the cost of exposing capital to risk. The purpose of this book is present to actuaries, regulators, and other interested parties a number of points of view to make it clear that this matter is not settled in the academic community at large. To this end, the various articles have been organized into two principle schools of thought.

Historically, the first school of thought is that the act of placing capital at risk only makes sense in the presence of a reward for so doing. That is, managers of underwriting businesses of all types are risk averse, and that risk aversion, whatever its nature, creates a demand for capital that leads to a reward for its use. This school of thought encompasses the actuarial theory of risk, as outlined by Karl Borch, Hans Bühlmann, and others. One implication is that profit standards should be expressed as ratios to premiums. The profit provision is not a function of the capital structure of the firm and there is no need to impute an investment of capital in support of the insurance.

Historically, the second school of thought is that all risk-taking is, in its essence, the same as making an investment. That is, managers of underwriting businesses of all types have the opportunity to use their capital to do other businesses, or to invest in the stocks of companies that make investments. This school of thought encompasses the financial theory of the cost of capital. One implication is that profit standards should be expressed as ratios to amounts of capital at risk. The profit provision is a function of the capital structure of the firm, or at least of some imputed capital in support of the insurance. This school of thought appears in key property-casualty insurance regulation, and is treated here first.

In this book, Stephen D'Arcy sets forth the financial theory of risk. Charles L. McClenahan sets forth the case for the actuarial theory of risk. The discussion is enlivened by the observations of other current writers in the field, each of whom presents a personal perspective.

Chapter 1, The Legal Perspective, by Judith Mintel, provides a brief history of the key legal decisions that set the stage for rate regulation today.

Chapter 2, Fundamental Building Blocks of Insurance Profitability Measurement, by Russell E. Bingham, makes an important contribution to any discussion of risk and return by pointing out the importance of careful accounting for the financial results on a group of policies. Accident-year accounting may be valuable for some regulatory purposes, but premium rates do not correspond to the results of a given accident year, so policy-year accounting is important for ratemaking purposes.

The discussion of methods that associate profit provisions with imputed investments of equity begins with Chapter 3, The Discounted Cash Flow Approach, by Stephen P. D'Arcy. D'Arcy introduces the basics of the Discounted Cash Flow (DCF) approach and shows the relationship to the formula for the net present value of a stream of financial flows.

Chapter 4, Cash Flow Models in Ratemaking, by Russell E. Bingham, shows the equivalence of two popular methods of DCF analysis under a reasonable set of assumptions.

Chapter 5, Rate of Return, by Frank D. Pierson, describes an application of DCF at a reinsurance company. Pierson explains the advantages of the concept of Allocated Risk Capital (ARC) and shows a linear relationship between the standard deviation of the policy's returns, the correlation of the policy's results with the portfolio as a whole, and a parameter for the security of the portfolio as a whole.

Chapter 6, Investment-Equivalent Reinsurance Pricing, by Rodney Kreps, develops a formula for the risk load by analogy with the financial theory of option pricing. Beginning with observations about yields on other investments, Kreps develops a risk charge that is not a function of imputed capital.

Chapter 7, Theoretical Premiums for Property and Casualty Insurance Coverage, by Ira Robbin, emphasizes the investor's point of view. In particular, this paper points out that the conservative nature of statutory accounting increases the cost of capital.

The discussion of methods that associate profit provisions with measures of loss and premium begins with Chapter 8, Insurance Profitability, by Charles L. McClenahan. McClenahan provides an introduction and overview of the return-on-premium perspective.

Chapter 9, The Confirmed Operating Return Approach, by Judith Mintel, shows the relationships between the legal requirements and the return-on-premium approaches.

Chapter 10, The Profit Provision, by Charles F. Toney II, emphasizes the importance of clarity and common sense in the process of rate regulation.

Chapter 11, The Cost of Capital: An Axiomatic Approach, which I wrote, links the return-on-premium approach to the foundations of micro-economics developed in the 1950's and 1960's. Risk loads that are consistent with simple axioms of good business behavior are a function of the risks underwritten and not a function of the capital structure of the insurance company.

In the preface to the first edition of The Capital Budgeting Decision in 1960, Harold Bierman, Jr., and Seymour Smidt wrote, "The purpose of this book is to present for an audience, which may be completely unfamiliar with the technical literature on economic theory or capital budgeting, a clear conception of how to evaluate investment proposals. The authors are convinced that the "present-value" method is superior to other methods....The early pages of the book show "cash payback" and "return on investment" may give incorrect results." Bierman and Smidt thought the answers were clear, but time has shown that they are not. Criticism of all of the methods has accumulated over the years. We hope the reader develops an appreciation of the high level of research and activity currently under way regarding the determination of appropriate standards for profit margins. Good science is denoted by controversy and growth as well as by the use of widely accepted models of the world.

Oakley E. Van Slyke
San Clemente, California
March, 1998

CHAPTER ONE
THE LEGAL PERSPECTIVE: APPROPRIATE PROFIT MARGINS IN PROPERTY & CASUALTY INSURANCE RATES

by Judith Mintel

OVERVIEW

The appropriate standard for determining profit margins for property and casualty insurance rates has been and is being influenced by lawyers, judges and insurance commissioners as well as investors, actuaries and economists. The contribution from the former groups is one that comes from quite a different perspective emphasizing legal and political considerations rather than financial or actuarial ones. Also, the articulation of the appropriate standards when originating from the legal/regulatory community is usually qualitative rather than quantitative. This often results in debates about how a qualitative legal standard should be translated and quantified into a particular profit margin in an insurance rate. The purpose of this chapter is to discuss some of the most prominent legal standards for determining insurance company profit margins and how those standards are evolving and affecting insurance pricing activities today.

STATUTORY AND CONSTITUTIONAL STANDARDS FOR PROFIT MARGINS

The common legal standards affecting profit margins in insurance rates are those contained in the insurance rate regulatory statutes in effect in a majority of states.[1] These provisions are:

> Rates shall not be excessive, inadequate, or unfairly discriminatory....
>
> Due consideration shall be given to... a reasonable margin for profit and contingencies.

Another important source for legal standards in this area is constitutional law. The Fifth Amendment to the United States Constitution (and similar provisions in most state

---

[1] There are a number of states that have enacted unique statutory or regulatory provisions that may either directly or indirectly affect the profit provision in insurance rates. For example, a few states have enacted requirements relating to the consideration of some or all of an insurer's investment income in the ratemaking process. Other states have adopted specific profit requirements (primarily affecting the personal auto insurance line) such as the excess profits statute in Florida or the "Clifford Formula" in New Jersey.

constitutions) prohibit government from taking the use of private property without providing for a hearing (due process of law) and paying just compensation. The 5th Amendment to the United States Constitution provides:

> No person shall be... deprived of life, liberty or property without due process of law; nor shall private property be taken for public use without just compensation.

The traditional statutory requirements for insurance rates were developed in 1946 as a part of the Model Prior Approval Act adopted by the National Association of Insurance Commissioners (NAIC). This model law grew out of the then current legal thinking relating to antitrust enforcement. Because the NAIC Prior Approval Rating Law authorized certain joint anti-competitive pricing activities by insurance companies through rating bureaus (cartels), the law also authorized the government regulator to prohibit the earning of monopoly profits by all insurers (including bureau members and nonmembers).

These legal requirements were based on the theory that government should be given the power to control insurance rates and profit margins because competition could not be relied on to do so. If a proposed rate was too low in relation to costs it was assumed to be an indication of attempted monopolization and predatory pricing; if the rate was too high, it was assumed to be an indication of the intent to earn monopoly profits. Competitive discipline on pricing decisions and profit margins was assumed not to be effective due to the legalization of joint pricing behavior. In other words, the legal theory underlying even the earliest insurance prior approval rating laws was similar to the legal theory underlying public utility rating laws, i.e., government control of prices was needed to prevent unreasonable restraints on trade and the extraction of monopoly profits in a non-competitive market.[2]

This similarity in underlying legal theory remains true today despite the very real and significant differences between the markets for most public utilities and insurance markets. One can argue that the competitive nature of insurance markets should obviate the need for direct government price controls. However, given the presence of insurance rate regulatory statutes, it is very difficult, if not impossible, to assert successfully in any legal forum that rate regulation common law principles are not applicable legal precedent for interpreting that law. This history helps explain why the legal precedent developed in the area of public utility price regulation has been and is now being used to help determine the appropriate legal standards for insurance company profit margins.

---

[2] The fact that many in the industry and regulatory ranks advocated legalization of joint pricing activities to enhance insurer solvency and keep in check the tendency towards ruinous competition does not affect the underlying legal theory of prior approval rate laws at least as it affects profit margins.

PUBLIC UTILITY COMMON LAW PRECEDENT

Today when an insurance rate case is briefed by lawyers before an administrative law judge, court or other tribunal, the precedent cited usually involves several public utility rate cases as well as insurance rate cases. The United States Supreme Court decision in Federal Power Commission v. Hope Natural Gas Co., 320 U.S. 591 (1944) is central to most arguments involving the appropriate profit margins for regulated entities including insurers. In the Hope case, the Supreme Court established certain basic principles governing the question of what constitutes "just compensation" as required by the 5th Amendment to the Constitution. It also tends to be central in arguments concerning whether the rate fixed or approved by government is "inadequate" or whether it fails to provide a "reasonable margin for profit" under the applicable statutory standards. Chief among the Hope principles is the requirement that the rate afford the regulated firm an opportunity to earn a fair and reasonable return and cover its cost of capital. As Justice Douglas explained:

> From the investor or company point of view it is important that there be enough revenue not only for operating expenses, but also for the capital costs of the business. These include service on the debt and dividends on the stock.... By that standard the return to the equity owner should be commensurate with returns on investments in other enterprises having corresponding risks. That return, moreover, should be sufficient to assure confidence in the financial integrity of the enterprise, so as to maintain its credit and to attract capital. (320 U.S. at 603.)

Hope adopted the views expressed earlier by Justice Brandeis in his opinion joined in by Justice Holmes in Southwestern Bell Telephone Co. v. Public Service Commission, 26 U.S. 276 (1923):

> The compensation which the Constitution guarantees an opportunity to earn is the reasonable cost of conducting the business. Cost includes not only operating expenses, but also capital charges. Capital charges cover the allowance, by way of interest, for the use of the capital, whatever the nature of the security issued therefore; the allowance for risk incurred; and enough more to attract capital.... A rate is constitutionally compensatory, if it allows to the utility the opportunity to earn the cost of the service as thus defined. (26 U.S. at 290.)

These early legal standards relating to profitability are ambiguous as to whether a Total Return Analysis[3] is the more appropriate approach from a legal standpoint or whether an Operating Return Analysis is required.[4] On the one hand, the language used by the Supreme Court seems to require an analysis that evaluates the riskiness of the business, an ability to compare returns among different industries and a method for determining a return on assets invested in the business. On the other hand, the language used often contains a clear distinction between operating expenses and capital charges implying the need for an analysis that separates the two and includes a positive operating return.

As the Hope doctrine has been interpreted by regulators, lawyers and judges in the ensuing years it has become clear that what the law guarantees is not the actual earning of a profit itself, but rather the opportunity to earn a fair and reasonable rate of return. Thus, inefficient companies or companies trying to sell products in a dying market are not guaranteed a profit by the presence of regulation. In Market Street Ry. v. Railroad Comm'n., 324 U.S. 548 (1945) the United States Supreme Court held that rate regulation need not guarantee a profit to a company trying to operate a business in a declining industry, the street car business. The Court allowed the rate regulator to restrict reasonable returns to the salvage value of the property rather than its acquisition cost. Justice Jackson wrote:

> [A] company could not complain if the return which was allowed made it possible for the company to operate successfully. (324 U.S. at 566.)

Likewise, in Permian Basin Area Rate Cases, 390 U.S. 747 (1968) Justice Harlan upheld the regulator's decision to impose area-wide benchmark rate caps for natural gas pipeline companies. The benchmark rates were calculated using a profit factor based on a

---

[3] Total Return Analysis means:

$$\frac{A+B+C}{D} = \frac{A+B_1+B_2+C}{D}$$

[4] Operating Return Analysis means:

$$\frac{A+B}{E} = \frac{A+B_1+B_2}{E}$$

Where:

A = Underwriting Profit/Loss

B = Investment Income (II) on current insurance operations ($B_1 + B_2$)

B_1= II on assets equivalent to loss and loss adjustment expense reserves.

B_2= II on assets equivalent to unearned premium reserves.

C = II on surplus properly converted to net worth.

D = Surplus properly converted to net worth.

E = Earned premium.

comparable earnings standard for the average pipeline company. (The profit factor allowed was a yield on equity of 12% in 1966.) The Court held:

> [N]o constitutional objection arises from the imposition of maximum prices merely because high cost operators may be more adversely affected than others, or because regulation reduces the value of the regulated property. (390 U.S. at 812.)

The natural gas pipeline companies had mounted a facial challenge to the area rate caps arguing that they were unconstitutional because the Commission had not set rates on an individual producer basis. The Permian Court upheld the maximum area rate procedure that the Commission had used stating that any rate selected by the Commission "from the broad range of reasonableness permitted by the Act cannot properly be attacked as confiscatory." The Court held:

> We do not suggest that maximum rates computed for a group or geographical area can never be confiscatory; we hold only that any such rates...intended to balance the investor and consumer interests are constitutionally permissible. (390 U.S. at 769.)

The Supreme Court also addressed the concern raised in Permian that the Commission failed to provide individualized relief from the group rates for a specific gas producer if the group rates were confiscatory in that particular, as-applied case. The Commission had declared that a producer would be permitted appropriate relief if it established that its "out-of-pocket expenses in connection with the operation of a particular well exceed its revenue from that well under the applicable area price."

In reviewing the Commission's regulations the Court of Appeals remarked that "out-of-pocket expenses are not defined and we do not know what they include." (390 U.S. 771 n. 35.) As a result, the Court of Appeal remanded the case to the Commission for a definition of the term "out-of-pocket expenses." The Supreme Court reversed holding that the Commission had not committed a fatal error in failing to define this term:

> We cannot now hold that, in these circumstances, the Commission's broad guarantees of special relief were inadequate or excessively imprecise. (390 U.S. at 772.)

Moreover, in Jersey Central Power & Light Co. v. FERC, 810 F.2d 1168 (D.C. Cir. 1987) Judge Robert Bork interpreted the Hope doctrine not to prohibit losses when those losses were due, not to government action, but instead due to bad management decisions, bad luck or inefficient operations. What the Jersey Central Court said was that "absent the sort of deep financial hardship described in Hope, there is no taking and hence no obligation to compensate just because a prudent investment has failed and produced no return." (810 F.2d at 1181 n. 3.)

In a more recent United States Supreme Court decision reaffirming the holding in the Hope case, Chief Justice Rhenquist in Duquesne Light Co. v. Barasch, 488 U.S. 299, 109 S.Ct. 609 (1989) identified three factors that critically impact the determination of whether the rate of return permitted by rate regulation is "fair and reasonable":

> The overall impact of the rate orders, then, is not constitutionally objectionable. No argument has been made that these slightly reduced rates jeopardize the financial integrity of the companies, either 1) by leaving them insufficient operating capital or 2) by impeding their ability to raise future capital. Nor has it been demonstrated that 3) these rates are inadequate to compensate current equityholders for [their] risk.... (488 U.S. at 312.)

The Court in Duquesne also suggested that the rate methodology selected for use by the regulator would not, in and of itself, subject a rate order to constitutional attack:

> The economic judgments required in rate proceedings are often hopelessly complex and do not admit of a single correct result. The Constitution is not designed to arbitrate these economic niceties. Errors to the detriment of one party may well be cancelled out by countervailing errors or allowances in another part of the rate proceeding. The Constitution protects the utility from the net effect of the rate order on its property. (109 S.Ct. at 619).

Thus, the constitutional analysis being used by the courts focuses on the end result of the rate order rather than the efficacy of any single ratemaking methodology; it is the impact of the rate order that matters and not the theory underlying the calculations.

As a result of these more recent court decisions, considerable debate has been generated concerning the meaning of statutory and constitutional standards as to what constitutes a fair and reasonable return under the law. For example, one major issue being debated today is the question of whether the cost of capital is the constitutional measure of a "fair rate of return" or whether there is some other lesser standard that passes constitutional muster. Another related issue is how to quantitatively express the "end result" of the allowed rate so that it can be determined whether the constitutional confiscation standard has been violated.

Currently, there are numerous articulations of the legal standard relating to allowable profit that arise from these public utility cases. Each of these articulations may create the same or different requirements depending on which standard or standards are applied and how they are interpreted. For illustration purposes, the following list is a simplified summary of some of the current legal standards:

COMMON LAW PUBLIC UTILITY PROFITABILITY STANDARDS SUMMARY

1. A rate must contain a provision for the capital costs of the business. (Hope)

2. A rate must contain a return to the equity owner commensurate with returns on investments in other enterprises having corresponding risks. (Hope)

3. A return must be included in the rate which allows the company to operate successfully. (Permian Basin)

4. A rate is not unconstitutional absent deep financial hardship. (Jersey Central)

5. A rate is not unconstitutional if the out-of-pocket expenses in connection with a particular portion of a firm's business do not exceed its revenue from the allowed rate for that portion of the business. (Permian Basin)

6. A rate is not unconstitutional if consumer interests are balanced against investor or company interests and rates are not exploitive. (Hope, Permian Basin)

7. The constitution guarantees the opportunity to earn a profit; it does not guarantee a profit itself. (Market Street)

8. The constitution protects a company from the consequences of the end result of a rate order, but does not dictate the use of any particular methodology. (Hope, Permian Basin, Duquesne)

INSURANCE COMMON LAW PRECEDENT

Courts examining profitability issues arising out of recent insurance rate cases have used the precedent and legal standards developed in the area of public utility rate regulation, but have added an insurance perspective that helps illuminate the practical effects of these standards on insurance rates. In Calfarm v. Deukmejian, 771 P.2d 1247 (1989) insurers challenged a statutory rate rollback of 20% enacted in Proposition 103 as facially unconstitutional and confiscatory. The statute did not allow relief from the rollback unless an insurer was threatened with insolvency. The California Supreme Court citing Hope held that "a rate may be confiscatory even though it does not threaten the insurer's solvency." (771 P.2d at 1254). It struck down the insolvency standard as violative of the Constitution and substituted a requirement that relief from the rollback must be granted an insurer if the rollback rates were "inadequate in that they did not contain a fair and reasonable rate of return." (771 P.2d at 1254).

In its discussion of the constitutional problems with the insolvency standard, the California Supreme Court recognized that rates are charged by state and by line of business whereas the insolvency standard referred to the financial condition of the entire company as a whole:

> Many insurers do substantial business outside of California or in lines of insurance within this state which are not regulated by Proposition 103.... In such a case the continued solvency of the insurer could not suffice to demonstrate that the regulated rate constitutes a fair return. (771 P.2d at 1254.)

Importantly, the California Supreme Court also recognized with disapproval that the original Proposition 103 insolvency standard encompassed the profits not only from current rates, but also from past rates:

> If an insurer had substantial net worth... it might be able to sustain substantial and continuing losses on regulated insurance without danger of insolvency.... [The rollback] rates which might be below a fair and reasonable level might compel insurers to return to their customers surpluses exacted through allegedly excessive past rates. But the concept that rates must be set at a less than a fair rate of return in order to compel the return of past surpluses is not one supported by precedent.... No case supports an unreasonably low rate of return on the ground that past profits were excessive. (771 P.2d at 1254.)

These standards articulated by the Calfarm Court which focus on a by-line, by-state profitability analysis, and which specifically exclude a rate which compels the return of "past surpluses", argue for a profitability analysis which looks at whether a rate is expected to produce a positive operating return.

An operating return approach is also one that seems to flow from the decision of the Ninth Circuit Court of Appeals in Guaranty National Ins. Co. v. Gates, 916 F.2d 508 (1990). In Gates the Federal Circuit Court of Appeals struck down a Nevada rollback statute because it "permitted only marginal or break-even rates." The Ninth Circuit noted that the Nevada rating law defined insurance rates as inadequate "if they are clearly insufficient, together with the income from investments attributable to them, to sustain projected losses and expenses in the class of business to which they apply." [Section 686B.050(3) Nev. Rev. Stat.] This Nevada statute clearly refers to a zero operating return.

The Federal Court concluded that the break-even operating return standard contained in the statute is not sufficient to guarantee the constitutionally required "fair and reasonable rate of return." Judge Levy wrote:

> From the investor or company point of view, it is important that there be enough revenue not only for operating expenses but also for the capital costs of the business.... Because Section 686B.050(3) specifically defines

> "inadequate" in a constitutionally unacceptable fashion, we may not simply sever the insolvency provision… as the California Supreme Court did in Calfarm. (916 F.2d at 515).

Even when a Court is upholding insurance rate regulation which uses a total rate of return methodology it is interesting that the legal articulation of the profitability standard applied seems to be more consistent with an operating return approach. In 20th Century Ins. Co. v. Garamendi, 878 P.2d 566 (1994) the California Supreme Court upheld the Commissioner's Proposition 103 rollback regulations[5] and the rollback ordered for 20th Century Insurance Company as legal based on its conclusion that 20th Century was able to "operate successfully during the period of the rate and subject to then-existing market conditions." Justice Mosk wrote:

> At least in the general case such as this, confiscation does indeed require "deep financial hardship" within the meaning of Jersey Central. Hence, it does not arise… whenever a rate does not "produce a profit which an investor could reasonably expect to earn in other businesses with comparable investment risks, and which is sufficient to attract capital." Profit of that magnitude is, of course, an interest that the producer may pursue but it is not a right that it can demand. It is "only one of the variables in the constitutional calculus of reasonableness."
>
> …This follows from the fact that under Hope, a regulated firm may claim that a rate is confiscatory only if the rate does not allow it to operate successfully…. Indeed, a rate can threaten confiscation only when it prevents the producer from "operating successfully" as that phrase is impliedly defined in prior opinions and is expressly used in this, viz., operate successfully during the period of the rate and subject to then existing market conditions. (878 P.2d at 617, 618.)

One way to interpret this language is that it is legally important to have a profit margin which is based on a total return analysis that identifies reasonable investor expectations and enables a comparison of insurance company returns with those in other industries. This evidence can be used to determine whether a proposed rate is excessive (i.e., outside the range of reasonableness on the high end). However, this analysis is not legally sufficient to determine whether a rate is inadequate or confiscatory (i.e., outside the range

---

[5] The Commissioner had adopted in regulations a profitability standard representing the "minimum constitutionally permitted rate of return" of 10% of a calculated "leverage norm." The 10% figure was derived from an historical analysis of the property and casualty insurance industry without reference to the returns in other industries of comparable risk or investor expectations. Leverage norms were developed to determine each company's surplus for use in converting the 10% return on equity to a percentage of premium that could be used directly in adjusting rate levels. The leverage norms were premium to surplus ratios derived by an arbitrary allocation of industry-wide actual surplus to line of business; an individual company's leverage norm was then calculated based on its own distribution of business.

of reasonableness on the low end). In order to determine whether a rate is confiscatory one must look not at investor returns or comparable earnings, but at whether the company is able to operate successfully during the period of the rate, to cover out-of-pocket costs and avoid deep financial hardship, however these terms might ultimately be defined.

There are a number of other reported insurance rate cases that uphold an operating return approach, but these cases do not have a constitutional dimension. The Courts simply apply a usually unique statutory provision requiring the use of an operating return. For example, in State ex. rel. Commissioner of Ins. v. North Carolina Rate Bureau, 261 S.E.2d 671 (1979) affirmed 269 S.E.2d 602 (1980) the North Carolina Courts held that it is not proper to consider investment earnings on capital or stockholder supplied funds in ratemaking although investment earnings from funds attributable to insurance operations is appropriate. The North Carolina rating law required consideration of "investment income earned or realized from unearned premium and loss and loss experience reserve funds generated from business within this state" in the rate approval process.

Likewise, Courts have upheld the insurance commissioner's decision to use an underwriting profit in the rates. In Insurance Department v. City of Philadelphia, 173 A.2d 811 (1961) the City, representing auto insurance consumers, argued that the profit factor used in ratemaking should be calculated as a percentage of invested capital and not as a percentage of earned premium. The Court upheld the Commissioner's order approving the rate change. It found that the use of the words "reasonable margin for underwriting profit" in the statute was intended to exclude investment income from consideration. The rejection by the Court of the ratemaking approach proposed by the City was based primarily on a finding that the statutory language constituted a legislative intent to distinguish between the competitive automobile insurance market and the provision of services by a monopoly public utility. As a result, it was found to be unnecessary to determine a return that could be compared with the returns in other industries because competition was assumed to be controlling the profit margin.

Moreover, Courts have addressed and upheld the insurance commissioner's ratemaking decisions when a total rate of return approach was used. In Attorney General v. Commissioner of Ins., 353 N.E.2d 745 (1976) the Massachusetts Commissioner rejected the use of a profit margin expressed as a percentage of premium as the "shoddiest component" of ratemaking and substituted a capital asset pricing model. The insurance rating law applicable to automobile insurance rates in Massachusetts provides that "due consideration shall be given to a reasonable rate of return on capital after provisions for investment income." The Court upheld the Commissioner's decision and approach to the profit provision based on the statutory language.

The foregoing discussion of the legal standards applicable to insurance profit margins should be adequate to communicate the fact that the legal and regulatory communities are no more in agreement on the appropriate approach to insurance rate profit provisions than are the actuarial and financial communities. Many regulators and legislatures prefer not to deal with the issue. Instead they rely on the competitive market to produce appropriate profit margins. A few regulators, legislatures and reviewing courts require an evaluation of rates using a total return analysis by finding it necessary to calculate the cost of capital and to compare insurance returns by line, by state with returns in other industries of comparable risk. Others focus on the return from current insurance operations and insist that any proper evaluation indicate whether this return is positive. Some seem to refer to more than one type of profit margin as they articulate the applicable legal standards.

CHAPTER TWO

FUNDAMENTAL BUILDING BLOCKS OF INSURANCE PROFITABILITY MEASUREMENT

By Russell E. Bingham

OVERVIEW

There are numerous approaches to the measurement of insurer profitability and ratemaking. On the surface, these approaches appear to be quite different since the results produced by them can, and often do, yield conflicting results. Certainly confusion is created when figures and results differ, and it is unclear as to the cause of the difference. This is especially true in the area of ratemaking, given the perspectives and agendas of the various parties involved. In order to assist in furthering the dialogue among interested parties, it is important that the sources of differences be understood. These differences can result from the data used, from the models used to process and present the data, from the assumptions used in the model, and from fundamentally different philosophical approaches.

Certain fundamental building blocks, successfully understood and employed, can provide a common, unifying structure which allows results produced by various models and approaches to be more readily compared. These building blocks provide a framework within which the differences in data, models, assumptions and philosophy can be argued to resolution.

The key building blocks, or principles, are:

- The existence of an accounting structure consisting of a fully integrated set of ***balance sheet, cash flow and income statements***.

- Differentiation between accounting by ***policy period***, the fundamental unit of insurance exposure, and accounting by ***calendar period***. Calendar period accounting is an aggregation of activity emanating from the current and previous policy periods.

- Recognition that much of what is reported as ***"actual" results*** in insurance accounting is based on estimation (e.g. IBNR) and that ***future development*** affecting subsequent calendar period balance sheet, cash flow and income statements is necessary to fully measure the ultimate financial results of a given policy period. Insurance is unique in that most of product costs are unknown at the time the product is priced and sold, and furthermore, "historical" policy period results, which form the basis for estimation of these costs, will not be fully known for some time.

- Using two valuation methods in which financials are viewed:
  - on a ***nominal*** basis, essentially using results as they develop and are reported over time, as well as
  - on a ***present value*** basis, which references all financials to a common point in time, by reflecting the time value of money.
- Identification and explanation of the key driving ***principles and philosophy***, as well as the ***parameters and statistics*** to be employed in the analysis. Understanding the meaning of the key assumptions and how they are derived along with the statistics used to present the results is critical to ratemaking and insurance financial analysis.

ACCOUNTING STRUCTURE

The existence of a fully integrated set of balance sheet, income and cash flow financial statements is invaluable whenever any form of analysis is to be performed. Their existence provides a fuller view of the financials embodied in any particular ratemaking or performance measurement process. In addition, questionable assumptions and inconsistencies are less likely to occur when these three perspectives are maintained and reviewed. Financial ratios used to determine profitability and rate of return are also derived from the relationships between variables in one or more of these three views. There seldom is a good reason not to build a financial model with these three critical perspectives.

POLICY PERIOD VS CALENDAR PERIOD

It is generally accepted that an understanding of calendar period incurred losses requires a breakdown into current and prior accident period contributions as presented by the Schedule P "triangles". Losses that are reported in any given calendar period emanate from accidents that occurred over the current accident period as well as possibly several prior accident periods. Calendar period losses, in and of themselves, may have little in common except the fact that their financial activity occurred during the same period. The losses could well have come from policies with differing exposures and pricing. In order to properly match insurance costs to premium revenue, losses need to be associated with the same period and exposures for which premiums were charged. This is critical to both the establishment of an historical ratemaking base and to the measurement of profitability.

It should be noted that "accident" period as a frame of reference is used for simplicity, however, "policy" period is the more appropriate classification, since this represents the real product unit of exposure. Of course, if all policies were of one year terms and effective on January 1, the results would be identical.

To set rates and measure financial performance of any given period, it is important that revenues and expenses be properly matched. Comparing premiums earned in 1995 with losses incurred in 1995, for example, may lead to improper results to the extent these losses arise out of policies sold (and rated) in years prior to 1995. The ideal solution is to expand the loss "triangle" concept to the complete package of balance sheet, income and cash flow statements, by policy period. In particular, the existence of surplus in this manner would render it possible to determine the ultimate profitability of any given policy period book of business (from the shareholder perspective).

Essentially, this ideal suggests that separate books be maintained for each policy period of exposure along with the policy period's respective contribution to calendar period reported financials that follow in time. Such books would clearly identify all elements of the particular book of business, such as revenue, expense and surplus committed and all manner of performance measures would be possible. The following schematic demonstrates this perspective.

TABLE 1

POLICY/CALENDAR PERIOD TRIANGLE

BALANCE SHEET, INCOME, CASH FLOW

	Calendar Period					
Policy		Historical		Future		Total
Period	1993	1994	1995	1996	1997	Ultimate
Prior	X	X	X	X	X	→ Sum
1993	X	X	X	X	X	→ Sum
1994		X	X	X	X	→ Sum
1995			X	X	X	→ Sum
1996				X	X	→ Sum
1997					X	→ Sum
	====	====	====	====	====	
Reported Calendar	Sum	Sum	Sum	Sum	Sum	

TIME FRAME OF ANALYSIS

Insurance, perhaps more than any other major business, involves pricing and selling of a product for which the major costs (loss) can only be estimated, and furthermore, the actual amount of which may not be known for many years to come. Whenever insurance financials are analyzed, it is important to understand that the view is of less than fully "developed" results. Older policy (or accident periods) may be largely resolved, but the closer one gets to the current time, the less this is so. Also, as noted in the previous section, the results reported in any given calendar period are an amalgamation of many different originating exposure periods.

Therefore, an important part of the analysis of insurance results is the proper slotting of calendar activity into the appropriate cell of the policy/calendar period development triangle, and the subsequent interpretation of the cumulative development pattern emerging. A major role of the actuary is to project the development of losses to their ultimate final estimated value based on these observed patterns.

Two important principles are involved:

- Historical, "actual" calendar results are a combination of current and previous policy periods.

- The results reported to date are incomplete and must be projected to ultimate by some technique. The greater the incompleteness in the reported results, such as in long tail lines of business, the greater the amount of additional development that must be projected to arrive at ultimate value.

It is vital that the ratemaking process both distinguish policy period historical cost from calendar period costs reported and that it further incorporate a method to project costs to their ultimate value, especially for more recent policy periods. It should be noted that a fundamental shortcoming of the rate filing process lies in the tendency of regulators to rely on financials as reported. There is a feeling of concreteness to them regardless of the fact that they may be significantly flawed for the reasons mentioned: they are an aggregate of several older policy periods and they are not fully developed. In essence, the policy/calendar period triangle must be filled out into the future for current and prior policy periods in order to provide a proper analytical foundation for ratemaking and financial analysis.

This point is so important that it bears repeating. ***Calendar period financial data (a main source of regulatory information) is fundamentally flawed, and at best can only be an approximate estimate of true current performance depending on the consistency of insurance exposures over time, the speed at which prior policy periods are resolved, and a relatively stable economic environment, especially as regards to interest rates and inflation.***

VALUATION METHODS

Reported results are on a nominal basis, that is to say, not discounted in terms of present value in any way. In the ratemaking process the focus is on the next period in the future for which the rates will apply. The financial profitability and rate of return for this business involves the development (and estimation) of calendar period activity many periods into the future. Since rates are being developed in the present there is a need to relate this future activity to the present in some way. Here the process of discounting comes into play whereby this future financial activity is adjusted for the time value of money. Discounted cash flow models are used for this purpose and, as a result, the value of profit and rate of return for this period is estimated in present value terms. Of course, additional assumptions relative to discounting are required to perform this accounting.

Although not explicitly stated, this process of discounting utilizes the financial "triangles" structure, by summarizing across the calendar period dimension for the particular future policy period for which rates are being developed. To fully judge the success of these models, it is necessary to maintain an historical record in the policy/calendar period triangle form (balance sheet, income and cash flow statements), which is seldom done.

PHILOSOPHY, PARAMETERS AND STATISTICS

Once the structural and valuation methodologies are established consistently, the differences that remain in ratemaking approaches are those truly of fundamental philosophical orientation. For example, should profitability be defined from the investor perspective and total rate of return on surplus be used, or should profitability be defined using a return on sales approach wherein surplus need not be assigned to lines of business. The parameters and statistics utilized in support of a particular position are driven largely by this orientation.

The differences in underlying fundamental philosophy influence the selection of parameter values and thus the final outcome.

PUTTING IT ALL TOGETHER

A "complete" approach to ratemaking and insurance financial analysis generally embodies all of the several building blocks mentioned. These include:

Structure

- the existence of supporting balance sheet, cash flow and income statements

- triangle structure differentiating policy (or accident) and calendar period dimensions.

Quantitative Approach

- focus on policy period dimension, including projections to ultimate value, in effect, "filling in" estimated future calendar period activity related to the given policy period

- valuation on both nominal and present value basis, again focusing on policy period dimension when constructing present value.

It is suggested that every financial model of insurance, whether to be used in ratemaking or measurement of profitability, should be all-inclusive of the above. ***Structurally*** the model should have balance sheet, cash flow and income statements which are available in triangle form, in the two dimensions of policy period by calendar period of **development**. ***Quantitatively*** the valuations need to focus on the policy period dimension inclusive of projections to ultimate and a method for determining the net present value of this policy period. Given these underpinnings, the remaining philosophical differences and parameter estimations can be addressed in a common format which should facilitate the discussion and resolution of differences.

Much of the confusion today exists needlessly because of a lack of common structure and quantitative approach.

> **Quite simply, if balance sheet, cash flow and income statements exist in a policy/calendar period triangle form, and if the policy period dimension is projected to ultimate and discounted to present value, the only remaining differences that need to be explained are in philosophy. In the end these are the only differences that matter.**

All forms of ratemaking and profitability measurement can benefit if these structural and quantitative principles are followed. Virtually all of the supposed different ratemaking "models", for example, can be reconciled to one another. Some of the apparent differences that remain are due more to the form of presentation than to fundamental philosophy. At a minimum it becomes possible to provide a focus on the true differences in philosophy and parameter assumptions that underlie each respective approach.

CHAPTER THREE
INTRODUCTION TO THE DISCOUNTED CASH FLOW APPROACH

By Stephen P. D'Arcy, FCAS

INTRODUCTION

The property-liability insurance industry has moved, by choice or otherwise, from a time when there was general agreement on a standard profit margin as a percentage of premium to a time when it is difficult to know what the profit margin truly is or should be. That we have not yet arrived at a point where there is a new consensus should be obvious, for then this book would not be necessary. This chapter aims to provide a simple introduction to the concept of discounted cash flow analysis, which is widely accepted in the field of finance as the proper approach in a variety of applications.

INSURANCE AND THE CAPITAL MARKETS

Assume that you have a significant sum of money available to invest and are considering your alternatives. The array of choices includes bonds of differing maturities and credit worthiness, equities with different dividends and price volatilities and an almost unlimited number of other investments in such categories as real estate, futures, and options. In addition, you have the opportunity to underwrite insurance. Viewed in this manner, it seems apparent that you would invest in the insurance business only if the return on your investment, which would include both underwriting and investment income, were commensurate with the other investment alternatives with similar risk characteristics available to you.

Although it could be argued that an insurance company does not really make the choice each year about whether to write insurance or instead simply to become an investment fund, that is, in essence, the choice that is being made in the capital markets. If the insurance industry is not earning a return high enough to compensate investors with a market level return (that rate paid on investments with similar risk characteristics), new capital will not be invested in insurance and the capital that can be withdrawn from the insurance industry will be. This trend will continue either until the industry has no capital remaining, an unfortunate possibility for Lloyd's of London right now, or until the return improves enough so investors are convinced that a competitive return will be earned.

Mutual insurance companies may appear to represent an entirely different form of financial institution, with a different set of objectives from proprietary insurers.

However, in essence, mutuals can be viewed as simply a combination contract or tied product, in which an individual's investment (as owner) and insuring (as policyholder) decisions are made together. If the cost of insurance becomes too high or the return on investment too low, the mutual will lose its business and its owners. Since the decisions are tied together, though, and the cost of searching for a new insurer and investment may turn out to be higher than searching for a single alternative alone, then the adjustment process to the appropriate level of earnings in a mutual may take longer than in a proprietary insurer. In addition, when a policyholder leaves a mutual company, capital contributed to the firm is, in practice, forfeited. This makes a difference in the investment decision. Also, there is evidence that management in a mutual insurer is less subject to the vicissitudes of a competitive economy than other forms of ownership.

Insurance is an extremely complex financial transaction, with stochastic payment streams that extend over many years, unique financial accounting provisions, a myriad of regulatory requirements, intricate tax regulations, a product susceptible to significant large losses and a market structure unlike any other industry. These factors combine to make it very difficult to measure the returns earned on the insurance business and the risk characteristics associated with these returns. In light of these difficulties, alternative methods for establishing profit margins are frequently used in the insurance business. To the extent that these models ignore investment income completely, they are fatally flawed, as the insurance business, which in general collects premiums well before losses are paid, functions as a financial intermediary and invests funds prior to disbursement. The rate of return earned on those funds is a vital component of the insurance transaction.

To the extent that the alternative models incorporate an historical investment income value, they are usable only as long as the investment markets do not deviate much from their historical levels. In stable financial times, interest rates and the market risk premium (the additional return earned by investment in a portfolio of equities that reflects the risk characteristics of the stock market as a whole) may remain fairly constant for decades. In that case, the profit margins determined based on historical financial values will be reasonably accurate. However, these models will not be appropriate when significant shifts occur in financial markets. Given the degree of volatility in interest rates and market returns recently, a model premised on stability is unlikely to be very reliable.

In this paper I will espouse the use of discounted cash flow analysis to establish the appropriate underwriting profit margins for property-casualty insurance. Discounted cash flow models are one of the forms of financial pricing models that combine underwriting and investment returns and also incorporate risk considerations in establishing the target return on capital figure. Other financial pricing models that have been used to establish underwriting profit margins include the Capital Asset Pricing Model and the Option Pricing Model. However, the Discounted Cash Flow approach is more robust than the Capital Asset Pricing Model, since it is not limited to valuing only systematic risk, and more intuitive, with the parameters more easily calculated, than the Option Pricing Model.

Essentially, the Discounted Cash Flow approach establishes a floor level for the underwriting profit margin at which the Net Present Value of writing the insurance policy is zero. An insurer would not write a policy if the underwriting profit margin were below that level. In a world of perfect competition and information, the industry underwriting profit margin would converge on that value. However, those assumptions are not necessary for the Discounted Cash Flow approach to be useful.

PRESENT VALUE AND NET PRESENT VALUE

The Present Value of a series of cash flows is:

$$PV = \sum_{t=1}^{n} \frac{CF_t}{(1+r)^t}$$

where CF = cash flow
t = time
r = discount rate

The Present Value calculation is generally performed only on the cash inflows from an investment, ignoring the outflows, which are the actual investment made in the project. The Net Present Value calculation considers both the inflows and outflows, and, since most projects require an up-front investment of capital at time zero, the Net Present Value calculation is:

$$NPV = \sum_{t=0}^{n} \frac{CF_t}{(1+r)^t}$$

When using the Net Present Value decision process, a firm should invest in a project that has a positive NPV and avoid any negative NPV projects. Thus, when applying the NPV approach to insurance, an insurer should only write a policy if the NPV is greater than zero.

The standard criticisms of the NPV approach are that cash flows are uncertain, there may be different views as to the proper discount rate and projects are assumed to be independent. The first two criticisms are assumed to be resolved by the market process. Because cash flows are uncertain, they are discounted at a rate that reflects this uncertainty rather than at the risk-free rate. Although there may be disagreement over the appropriate interest rate to use for discounting, as there are differences in opinion in valuing any asset, the market clearing rate, the rate that balances supply and demand, is the rate to use. This assumption works well for widely traded assets, but approximations are needed to value projects that are not publicly traded. The third criticism, that projects are really not independent, is valid. The cash flows included in the valuation of any one project should reflect the impact on other projects as well. However, this is a difficult task to accomplish.

To begin with an overly simplified example, in order to focus on the methodology involved in the NPV approach, assume that you have the opportunity to invest \$100 million in insurance for one year. Your \$100 million investment will allow you to write \$200 million of premiums, on one year policies that are all effective the same day, for a line of business that settles all claims at the end of one year. Thus, there will be no unearned premium or loss reserves at the end of the year. The expense ratio on this business will be 25 percent and all expenses will be paid when the policies are written. If two further unrealistic assumptions are made, first that the losses are known with certainty, so you assume no risk in writing these policies, and second that all capital is invested in risk-free assets, then all cash flows can be discounted at the risk-free rate. The NPV calculation for this decision is:

$$NPV = -S + \frac{(S + P(1 - ER))r_f}{1 + r_f} + \frac{P(1 - ER - LR) + S}{1 + r_f}$$

where S = Investment (Surplus)
P = Premiums
ER = Expense Ratio
LR = Loss Ratio
r_f = Risk-Free Interest Rate

If, for example, this business could be written at a 75 percent loss ratio (including loss adjustment expenses), and the one year risk-free interest rate is 7 percent, then the NPV of this business would be:

$$NPV = -100 + \frac{(100 + 200(1 - .25)).07}{1.07} + \frac{200(1 - .25 - .75) + 100}{1.07} = 9.81$$

This calculation indicates that the investor would increase the value of his or her holdings by \$9.81 million by writing this business. Thus, this is an investment that should be undertaken. The discounted cash flow approach can also be used to determine the lowest underwriting profit margin that would be profitable for an insurer by solving for the underwriting profit margin at which the *NPV* is zero. Any underwriting profit margin above that value would have a positive *NPV*. The business should not be written at the zero *NPV* underwriting profit margin, or at any lower value. For this example, the break-even underwriting profit margin is negative 5.25 percent. Thus, the business should be written as long as the loss ratio is less than 80.25 percent.

This example assumed that there was no risk to either the underwriting or the investments. However, the insurance transaction obviously entails risk and that must be incorporated in the calculation. One method of incorporating risk in a financial transaction is to utilize a risk-adjusted discount rate. For example, assume that an investment has an expected cash flow of $100 at the end of one year, and the riskiness of the outcomes is such that the market requires a 12 percent discount rate, as opposed to a risk-free 7 percent rate. In this case, the Present Value of the cash flow is:

$$PV = \frac{100}{1.12} = 89.29$$

The $100 is divided by 1.12, which discounts for both the riskiness of the cash flow and the time value of money. Since we know that the time value of money, for a risk-free investment, is 7 percent, then the adjustment for risk is:

$$\text{Adjustment for Risk} = \frac{1.12}{1.07} = 1.0467$$

CERTAINTY-EQUIVALENT VALUES

The Certainty-Equivalent Value of a risky cash flow is the amount that is just large enough that an investor would be indifferent between receiving the Certainty-Equivalent Value and receiving the results of the risky cash flow. In this example, the Certainty-Equivalent cash flow one year from now is:

$$CEQ = \frac{100}{1.0467} = 95.54$$

This amount, $95.54, is termed the Certainty-Equivalent of the risky cash flow with an expected value of $100 since the investor is considered indifferent between the expected value of $100 and $95.54 for certain, each payable at the end of one year. The Present Value of this Certainty-Equivalent is:

$$PV = \frac{95.54}{1.07} = 89.29$$

This is the same as the Present Value when discounted for both risk and the time value of money simultaneously. The advantage of the Certainty-Equivalent method is that the risk adjustment and the time value of money adjustment are separated, rather than combined. This makes the adjustments easier to understand and usable in situations where the combined method is not feasible.

The Certainty-Equivalent method can be applied to the *NPV* insurance calculation with risk introduced into both the investment and underwriting aspects of the business. First, the insurer might elect to invest in risky, rather than risk-free securities. In that case, the numerator of the second term of that equation would be $(S + P(1 - ER))r$ instead of

$(S + P(1 - ER))r_f$, where r is the expected rate of return on the risky assets. Then, the denominator would have to reflect the risk associated with risky investments. This adjustment is not straightforward, since the initial investment has, in essence, been leveraged, creating greater risk, and therefore requiring a greater increase in the discount rate than the increase in expected return would generate.

However, the Certainty-Equivalent amount of that risky investment outcome is, by definition, $(S + P(1 - ER))r_f$. The financial markets equate the risky outcome with this risk-free outcome, since both represent the current market rates of return. Thus, the second step in the calculation, dividing the Certainty-Equivalent by the risk-free rate, yields the same result as calculated when there is no risk.

Incorporating underwriting risk has a definite effect on the results, though. Returning to the situation in which the expected loss ratio is 75 percent, the expected losses are $150 million. The Certainty-Equivalent of this value is the amount that would make the insurer indifferent between that certain payment and the uncertain amount that has an expected value of $150 million. Obviously this amount exceeds $150 million. Any insurer would gladly pay, for example, $145 million for certain in lieu of losses that are uncertain but with an expected value of $150 million. Remember that these payments are contemporaneous, both being made at the end of one year. The Certainty-Equivalent amount depends on the riskiness of the loss payments. The greater the chance of a significant loss in excess of $150 million, for example from a natural disaster, the larger the Certainty-Equivalent value will be. The adjustment cannot be looked up in a financial newspaper, as interest rates are, as insurance losses are not widely traded assets. An appropriate value for the Certainty-Equivalent would be what payment a reinsurer would be willing to accept at the end of one year in return for the agreement to pay whatever the losses turned out to be at that time. Let's assume that the Certainty-Equivalent value is $160.5 million, which means that the insurer is indifferent between the risky loss payout value with an expected value of $150 million and a certain payout of $160.5 million. In this case, the NPV of the insurance business is:

$$NPV = -100 + \frac{(100 + 200(1 - .25)).07}{1.07} + \frac{200 - 50 - 160.5 + 100}{1.07} = 0$$

Therefore, simply by reflecting the riskiness of underwriting in this example, the NPV changes from $9.81 million to zero, going from an investment that an individual would make to one to which an investor would be indifferent.

CONCLUSION

Applying the Net Present Value approach to insurance pricing creates many additional complications beyond determining the Certainty-Equivalent of the losses. One major complication involves accounting for taxes, as the insurance transaction exposes the investor to an additional layer of taxation that would not be incurred if an investor elected simply to invest capital in securities rather than writing insurance. Also, insurance transactions span many years, so the timing of capital inflows and outflows is not clear cut. Additionally, determining the correct amount invested is difficult, as statutory accounting distorts the economic value of an insurer. These and other difficulties have, to date, hindered the development of a widely accepted financial pricing technique for property casualty insurance, leading to the adoption of alternative techniques that ignore investment income or make an arbitrary adjustment for investment income. Despite the obstacles to developing a financial pricing model, this approach is the only one that can provide insurers with the information they need to price business correctly in volatile financial conditions. Thus, the work goes on to perfect such an approach.

CHAPTER FOUR

CASH FLOW MODELS IN RATEMAKING: A REFORMULATION OF MYERS-COHN NPV AND IRR MODELS FOR EQUIVALENCY[1]

by Russell E. Bingham

SUMMARY

The Myers-Cohn Net Present Value model and NCCI's IRR model are the two leading cash flow models used in ratemaking. This paper presents simple parameter and structural changes which demonstrate their equivalency. The "fair" premium produced by both models is shown to be identical given rational and consistent rules for setting parameter values, control of the flow of surplus, and discounting.

A byproduct of the structural changes proposed in the models is a rate of return that measures operating profitability. This "Operating Rate of Return" measures the insurance risk charge implicit in the ratemaking process in the form of a rate of return, yet it avoids the need to allocate surplus to lines of business. It is suggested as a replacement for the Return on Premium statistic.

Finally, ratemaking implications are discussed involving comparison of the liability beta and the equity beta, key parameters used in the Myers-Cohn and IRR models, respectively, which lead to determination of premium levels.

[1] Greg Taylor has also explored the relationships between the Myers-Cohn and the internal rate of return methods. "Fair Premium Rating Methods and the Relations Between Them," The Journal of Risk and Insurance, 1994 Vol. 61, No. 4, 592-615.

OVERVIEW

In recent years discounted cash flow models have gained in prominence as a ratemaking methodology and are often recommended by theoreticians and practitioners in the insurance field. The two predominant variations of cash flow models are the Myers-Cohn (MC) net present value (NPV) model, as used in Massachusetts, and the NCCI internal rate of return (IRR) model, used in many state workers compensation rate filings. Recent articles have discussed these two variations in detail and have further demonstrated the conditions under which they produce equivalent results. (See references (1), (3) and (11).)

The purpose of this paper is to suggest simple and straightforward modifications to these models in order to enhance their usage and to eliminate the unnecessary confusion that has existed as to the "differences" in these models when, in reality, there are none when the same parameters and assumptions are used. References (3) and (4) provide a more detailed background on the concepts and formulas which form the foundation for the material to be presented here.

The Myers-Cohn model is structured at an operating income level, that is, it deals with the present value of income from underwriting and from the investment only of policyholder provided funds. Formally, it does not provide a rate of return, and, by excluding surplus (except to reflect the tax on surplus related investment income when the "fair" premium is derived), it does not produce total net income and total rate of return. The NCCI model, in contrast, focuses primarily on the net cash flows to the shareholder, and the IRR that results, and it does not provide an operating return to measure the performance of insurance operations alone. The present form of each of these models, in terms of construction and underlying assumptions, makes it difficult to compare the results produced by them.

The modifications to be suggested here can be divided into a first group that is simply structural in nature to bring the models into alignment with each other and a second group that has to do with the parameter assumptions in order to establish consistency in application. The two most important technical points have to do with the use of after-tax discount rates, rather than before-tax rates, and the use of a liability-to-surplus leverage ratio to control shareholder surplus flows over time. As a result of these changes, each revised model will provide a clear statement of the separate rates of return to the policyholder, to the company from insurance operations, and to the shareholder. There will be a clear and identifiable linkage between the assumptions and results of both models, and income and rates of returns will be equivalent.

This article will begin by explaining the modifications required of the MC model to provide a NPV total rate of return. This will be followed by the modifications required of the IRR model to provide a rate of return that parallels the traditional MC operating level view, although the model is fine as is if the only objective is to produce a total rate of return to the shareholder. Essentially, MC will be expanded whereas IRR will be broken down to a finer level of detail.

The balance sheet corresponding to the underlying cash flows assumed by the models will be brought into the discussion since policyholder liabilities and surplus play an important role in the rate of return measurement process. The important linkage of surplus to liabilities will be discussed, as well, describing how both the initial surplus and its subsequent release to the shareholder should be governed by the nature of the insurance cash flows over a multi-year time frame.

Three rates of return are presented in the paper: (1) ***Underwriting Return*** (cost of policyholder supplied funds), (2) ***Operating Return*** (the charge to the policyholder for the transfer of underwriting risk to the company) and (3) ***Total Return*** to the shareholder. The Operating Return is presented as an alternative to the Return on Premium statistic preferred by those in the industry who have an aversion to the allocation of surplus and total return.

As a last point, the implications for ratemaking will be discussed. It will be shown that the premium determined by both the "reformulated" Myers-Cohn and IRR agree and the economic rationale for this. Of particular interest is the underlying connection between two critical parameters of the models: the liability beta, used by Myers-Cohn to establish the risk-adjusted discount rate for calculation of the "fair" premium, and the equity beta, used by the IRR approach to determine the cost of capital target return. Formulae are presented for the fair premium and the betas which, in the absence of measured market data, are used to demonstrate the (theoretical) relationships among the equity and liability betas, leverage and other variables.

Since the term "fair premium" is used often in the context of Myers-Cohn, definitions are offered below relative to both Myers-Cohn and IRR.

A premium is considered to be "fair" in the Myers-Cohn sense if the risk-adjusted total rate of return that results from use of this premium equals the risk-free rate.

A premium is considered to be "fair" in the IRR sense if the total rate of return that results from use of this premium equals the cost of capital.

This paper will demonstrate how the Myers-Cohn and IRR models, given equivalently defined parameters and model assumptions, produce an identical fair premium.

Myers-Cohn Net Present Value Model: Reformulation

The traditional MC model format as shown in reference (9) is as follows:

$$P = PV(L) + PV(UWPT) + PV(IBT)$$

This states that the fair premium, *P*, is equal to the sum of the present value of the losses, *L*, the tax on underwriting profit, *UWPT*, and the tax on investment income derived from the investable balance, *IBT*. The investable balance includes all policyholder liabilities (net of premium, loss and expense) and surplus. Note that underwriting expense is combined with loss as total liabilities in the example in the cited reference.

It is suggested that the discount rates be adjusted for risk (i.e. uncertainty), particularly the rate applicable to losses. No mention is made as to whether discount rates are on a before-tax or after-tax basis.

This traditional format will be followed to some degree, but extended to two periods and with slightly modified assumptions. A group of policies produce a premium, *P*, which is collected without delay (at time 0). Expenses, *E*, are $0. Losses, *L*, total $1,000 dollars and are paid at the end of two years. Taxes on underwriting and investment will be assumed to be paid without delay. In the original reference presentation underwriting taxes were assumed to have a one year delay in their payment. The tax loss discount (TRA 86) will be excluded for simplification.

Surplus will be set at each point in time to an amount equal to L/F, where F is the liability/surplus leverage factor. In the reference (9) previously cited, *S* was set equal to *P* for the single period example presented.

The following specific modifications to the traditional MC model are suggested to produce a total rate of return and permit an alignment with a similarly modified NCCI model.

STRUCTURAL CHANGES

1. Introduce surplus flows into the model, including related investment income.
2. Separate and clearly delineate income from (1) underwriting, (2) investment of policyholder funds, and (3) investment of shareholder surplus.
3. Construct balance sheets and income statements, valued on both a nominal and a present value basis, given the respective cash flows. The present value of liabilities and surplus are of particular importance.

4. Discount all flows using after-tax rates, whether risk-free or risk-adjusted rates.

5. Develop rate of return measures from the net present value income components (underwriting, operating income, and total income) by forming a ratio to the relevant balance sheet liability item. Although "fair" premiums are determined using risk-adjusted discount rates, display net present value calculations both ***with*** and ***without*** risk-adjustment to allow comparison to results produced via Internal Rate of Return.

6. Discount surplus and underwriting taxes also on a risk-adjusted basis to the degree they are influenced by losses. Surplus, since it is determined by use of a leverage ratio relative to liabilities inclusive of loss, and underwriting taxes, are both affected by loss and must also be risk-adjusted for the portion so affected. As in the case of losses, display net present value calculations both with and without risk-adjustment.

PARAMETER/OPERATIONAL CHANGES

1. Control surplus flows through a linkage with liabilities, both with respect to amount and timing.

2. Distribute operating earnings in proportion to the liability exposure over the period for which exposures exist. Essentially this rule distributes operating earnings in proportion to the loss reserve over time.

The use of an after-tax rate for discounting is critical, since a true economic present value cannot be determined unless the need to pay taxes is recognized. Furthermore, the fact that taxes are paid shortly after (investment) income is earned must also be reflected. This means that "inside-buildup" discount calculations, wherein before-tax rates are used with taxes determined in a single final step, is incorrect. In addition, use of an after-tax rate is necessary to bring the NPV measurements of income and return into sync with the IRR, in which use of an after-tax discount is implicit. The issue of after-tax discounting is discussed in more detail in the Appendix.

While the risk-adjusted discount rates may be used to calculate a "fair" premium, an alternative view is to focus on the total return instead. Using the same premium, when net present values are calculated without risk adjustment, the treatment of risk is framed in the context of establishment of a fair total return target, rather than as a discussion of how to risk-adjust losses. It is for this reason that present values are to be calculated both with and without risk adjustment. As will be shown in the examples, ***the risk-adjusted NPV rate of return will always equal the risk-free rate, and the NPV rate of return, not risk-adjusted, will equal the targeted cost of capital as calculated by the IRR***.

Exhibit I presents the derivation of the "fair" premium that results from this reformulated Myers-Cohn approach - from the use of after-tax discounting and the control of surplus via its linkage to liabilities. In this example interest rates are 10%, the tax rate is 35%, and a risk adjustment of 2.0%, before-tax (i.e. 1.3% after-tax) is made when discounting. A liability/surplus ratio of 4 to 1 is used to determine the level of surplus. The premium in this example is $876.63. As stated previously, premiums and taxes are assumed to have no delay in their receipt or payment.

EXHIBIT I

DERIVATION OF "FAIR" PREMIUM WITH AFTER-TAX DISCOUNTING

P =	PV(L)	903.60	$L/(1 + R - R_L)^N$ $1000/(1 + 0.065 - 0.013)^2$
	+ PV(UWPT)	-43.18	$T[P/(1 + R)^{N_T} - L/(1 + R - R_L)^{N_T}]$ $0.35[876.6/(1+0.065)^0 - 1000/(1+0.065-0.013)^0]$
	+ PV(IBT)	16.22	$T\,Rb\,S[(1 - 1/(1 + R - R_L)^N/(R - R_L)]$ $(0.35)(0.10)(250)[1-1/(1+0.065-0.013)^2/(0.065-0.013)$
"Fair" Premium Equals		**876.63**	

P:	Premium	*Rb*:	Interest Rate, Before-Tax
L:	Loss	*R*:	Interest Rate, After-Tax
N:	Loss Payment Date	R_L:	Risk Discount Adjustment, After-Tax
T:	Tax Rate	*F*:	Liability / Surplus Leverage factor
N:	Under. Tax Payment Delay	*S*:	Initial Surplus Contribution (L/F)

UWPT: Underwriting Profit Tax

IBT: Investable Balance Investment Income Tax

Notes: Due to After-Tax Discounting $PV(IBT)$ reduces to simply tax on investment income derived from the investable surplus balance.

Liability/Surplus Relationship implies Surplus level affected by risk adjustment.

Exhibit II presents a summarized balance sheet and income statement for this example, following conventional accounting rules. A two-period total and net present values, both with and without risk adjustment, are also shown for some items.

EXHIBIT II

BALANCE SHEET AND INCOME STATEMENT
(TWO PERIOD EXAMPLE)

	PERIOD				NPV Not Risk	NPV Risk
	0	1	2	Total	Adjusted	Adjusted
BALANCE SHEET (Ending)						
Total Assets	1,170	1,209	0	2,378	2,164	2,206
Loss Reserve	1,000	1,000	0	2,000	1,821	1,854
Retained Earnings	-80	-41	0	-122	-112	-112
Shareholder Surplus	250	250	0	500	455	464
Liabilities/Surplus	4.0	4.0	0			
INCOME AFTER-TAX						
Underwriting Income	-80	0	0	-80		
Investment Income						
Loss Reserves		65	65	130		
Retained Earnings		-5	-3	-8		
Total Operating	-80	60	62	42		
Investment Income						
Shareholder Surplus		16	16	32		

NET PRESENT VALUE INCOME AND RATE OF RETURN

The steps necessary to structure the model to produce total income and rate of return are recapped in Exhibits IIIa and IIIb (following page 35). Exhibit IIIa presents the calculations using a risk adjustment, and Exhibit IIIb presents them without the risk adjustment. First NPV Operating Income is calculated as:

$$\text{NPV Operating Income}(OI) = PV(P) - PV(L) - PV(UWPT)$$

The following is an alternative, yet equivalent, form of presentation for this operating income:

$$\text{Underwriting Income}(\text{UI}) + \text{Policyholder Funds Investment Income Credit}(IIC)$$

The use of the term "credit" is to reinforce the fact that this is the present value of investment income to be earned in the future. The net present value of income is calculated with risk-adjustment and without risk-adjustment (i.e. R_L is set to "0").

To include investment income on surplus it is necessary to simply add this to the formula as follows:

$$\text{NPV Total Income}(TI) = \text{Operating Income} + \text{Surplus Investment Income Credit}$$

The investment income on surplus is the present value of investment income to be earned on surplus in the future. Here surplus is set initially and then maintained over time using a given the liability/surplus leverage factor. Note that when losses are risk-adjusted $(R_L > 0)$ that surplus is implicitly risk-adjusted as well.

In order to permit the calculation of rates of return from operations and to the shareholder, the balance sheet "investment" upon which these returns are earned is needed. These items, NPV Operating Liabilities and NPV Surplus, are as shown.

It should be noted that all formulas presented are simplified due to the example selected, especially the assumption that all losses are to be paid in a single payment at the end of two years. In application, actual cash flows occurring over multi-periods each need to be discounted and summed to determine present value.

Three rates of return are of interest:

1. the underwriting rate of return on the assets corresponding to the liabilities assumed by the company when writing this business (i.e. the cost to the company of policyholder supplied funds),

2. the operating return to the company on the assets corresponding to the same policyholder liabilities assumed, including investment income on policyholder funds, (i.e. the insurance risk charge to the policyholder for the transfer of insurance risk to the company), and

3. the rate of return to the shareholder.

Each of these three rates of return is calculated by dividing a particular income item by its respective balance sheet liability (or its matching asset commitment). These are summarized below:

The underwriting return on liabilities, the cost of policyholder supplied funds to the company, is the ratio:

$$\text{Underwriting Return} = \text{NPV Underwriting Income}/\text{NPV Policyholder Liabilities}$$

The operating return on liabilities, the risk charge to the policyholder, is the ratio:

$$\text{Operating Return} = \text{NPV Operating Income}/\text{NPV Policyholder Liabilities}$$

Operating income is the sum of underwriting income and investment income on policyholder funds. Total return to the shareholder also includes investment income on surplus and is the ratio:

$$\text{Total Return on Surplus}(\text{ROS}) = \text{NPV Total Income}/\text{NPV of Surplus}$$

It is important to note that net present value of surplus is the sum of the amounts of surplus committed over the period of years, in present value terms. As mentioned previously, the control of this surplus flow is critical. Use of the liability/surplus leverage ratio over time is necessary to produce a result wherein the ROS equals the IRR. Also, as will be shown later, the annual income distribution to the shareholder will also equal this rate in each period.

The cost of policyholder supplied funds represents the rate of return the company pays to the policyholder on the pure underwriting related flows with the transfer of insurance risk to the company. The investment income on these flows will then accrue to the company's benefit. The net insurance charge to the policyholder reflects the sum of the underwriting cost, offset by the gain on investments realized by the company. Viewed mathematically (and using the data in Exhibit IIIB), the cost of policyholder funds of -4.4% plus the market rate of return on investments of 6.5% equals the insurance risk charge of 2.1%. In essence, the company earns the excess of the risk-free interest rate over the cost of funds paid to the policyholder in exchange for assuming the underwriting risk embodied in the transaction.

EXHIBIT IIIA

NET PRESENT VALUE INCOME, BALANCE SHEET AND RATE OF RETURN DEFINITIONS, FORMULAS AND CALCULATIONS **WITH** RISK ADJUSTMENT

INCOME ITEMS	FORMULAS
Underwriting Income	$(P-L)(1-T)$ $(876.63-1{,}000)(1-0.35)=-80$
Operating Income	$PV(P)-PV(L)-PV(UWPT)=P-L/(1+R-R_L)^N-T(P-L)$ $876.63-1{,}000/(1+0.065-0.013)^2-(0.35)(876.63-1{,}000)$ $(P-L)-T(P-L)/(1+R)^N+L\left(1-1/(1+R-R_L)^N\right)$ $(876.63-1{,}000)-(0.35)(876.6-1{,}000)/(1+0.065)^0$ $+1{,}000\left(1-1/(1+0.065-0.013)^2\right)$ = Underwriting Income + Investment Income Credit on Policyholder Liabilities $-80+96=16$
Surplus Investment Income	R(Surplus) $(0.065)(464)=30.16$
Total Income	Operating Income + Investment Income on Surplus $16+30=46$
BALANCE SHEET ITEMS	
Policyholder Liabilities	$L\left(1-1/(1+R-R_L)^N\right)/(R-R_L)$ $1{,}000\left(1-1/(1+0.065-0.013)^2\right)/(0.065-0.013)=1854$
Surplus	$S\left(1-1/(1+R-R_L)^N\right)/(R-R_L)$ $250\left(1-1/(1+0.065-0.013)^2\right)/(0.065-0.013)$
RATES OF RETURN	
Underwriting Return on Liabilities (UROL) (Cost of Policyholder-Supplied Funds)	Underwriting Income / Policyholder Liabilities $-80/1{,}854=-4.3\%$
Operating Return on Liabilities (ROL) (Risk Charge to Policyholder)	Operating Income / Policyholder Liabilities $16/1{,}854=0.9\%$
Total Return on Surplus (ROS) (Shareholder Return)	Total Income / Surplus $46/464=10.0\%$ $=(ROL)$(Liability/Surplus) $+R$ $0.9\%(4)+6.5\%=10.0\%$

EXHIBIT IIIB

NET PRESENT VALUE INCOME, BALANCE SHEET AND RATE OF RETURN DEFINITIONS, FORMULAS AND CALCULATIONS **WITHOUT** RISK ADJUSTMENT

INCOME ITEMS	FORMULAS
Underwriting Income	$(P-L)(1-T)$ $(876.63-1{,}000)(1-0.35)=-80$
Operating Income	$PV(P)-PV(L)-PV(UWPT)=P-L/(1+R)^N-T(P-L)$ $876.63-1{,}000/(1+0.065)^2-(0.35)(876.63-1{,}000)$ $(P-L)-T(P-L)/(1+R)^N+L\left(1-1/(1+R)^N\right)$ $(876.63-1{,}000)-(0.35)(876.6-1{,}000)/(1+0.065)^0+1{,}000\left(1-1/(1+0.065)^2\right)$ = Underwriting Income + Investment Income Credit on Policyholder Liabilities $-80+118=38$
Surplus Investment Income	R(Surplus) $(0.065)(455)=29.58$
Total Income	Operating Income + Investment Income on Surplus $38+30=68$

BALANCE SHEET ITEMS

Policyholder Liabilities	$L\left(1-1/(1+R)^N\right)/R$ $1{,}000\left(1-1/(1+0.065)^2\right)/0.065=1821$
Surplus	$S\left(1-1/(1+R)^N\right)/R$ $250\left(1-1/(1+0.065)^2\right)/0.065=455$

RATES OF RETURN

Underwriting Return on Liabilities (UROL) (Cost of Policyholder-Supplied Funds)	Underwriting Income / Policyholder Liabilities $-80/1821=-4.4\%$
Operating Return on Liabilities (ROL) (Risk Charge to Policyholder)	Operating Income / Policyholder Liabilities $38/1821=2.1\%$
Total Return on Surplus (ROS) (Shareholder Return)	Total Income / Surplus $68/455=14.9\%$ $=(ROL)$(Liability/Surplus) + R $2.1\%(4)+6.5\%=14.9\%$

"FAIR" PREMIUM EXAMPLES: THE EFFECT OF TAXES AND RISK ADJUSTMENT

It is interesting to observe how the modified fair premium determined in the manner shown produces a logical result in terms of rate of return from operations and to the shareholder as tax rates and the risk adjustment vary. Four examples are presented in Exhibit IV. Example 4 is the example used above.

Example 1 is without tax and without risk adjustment. The fair premium is $826.45, corresponding to an operating return of 0%, and the total return is 10%. ***When there is no risk, the return to the shareholder is simply the risk-free rate of 10%.***

Example 2 is with taxes at 35% and without risk adjustment. The fair premium increases to $842.45, the operating return is 0.9%, and the total return is 10%. The increased premium exactly covers the amount of taxes on the investment income from surplus necessary to provide a before-tax return to the shareholder. ***The shareholder is not responsible for payment of any taxes incurred within the insurance entity, and this is covered by the increased policyholder premium.*** Again, since there is no risk to the shareholder, the return to the shareholder is the risk-free rate of 10%.

Example 3 is presented to demonstrate what happens if the tax on the surplus related investment income is not included in premiums. This example, with taxes at 35% and without risk adjustment, is similar to Example 2, but the present value of the tax on the investment income from the surplus balance has been excluded from the determination of the fair premium. The premium declines to $817.94. The operating return is 0% and the total return is 6.5% to the shareholder. In this case the shareholder will receive only an after-tax rate or return. This demonstrates that ***the common definition of "break-even" as "0" operating return is not break-even from an investor's standpoint.***

The break-even return to the investor must be equivalent to a before-tax rate of return for it to be comparable to other investment opportunities. An insurance company must run above "0" operating return to be at break-even.

Example 4 is with taxes at 35% and with a risk adjustment of 2.0% before-tax, 1.3% after-tax. The premium increases to $876.63 to cover the added risk related to the uncertainty of the loss. This is the example presented earlier. Example 4A, utilizes this same fair premium but simply displays the results without use of the risk adjustment in the calculation of the net present values.

EXHIBIT IV

MODIFIED "FAIR" PREMIUM AND NET PRESENT VALUE INCOME, BALANCE SHEET AND RATES OF RETURN WITH VARYING TAX RATES AND RISK ADJUSTMENT

	Examples				
Assumptions & "Fair" Premium	1	2	3	4	4A
Tax Rate	0	35%	35%	35%	35%
Risk Adjustment(Before Tax)	0.00%	0.00%	0.00%	2.00%	set to 0
"Fair" Premium	826.45	842.45	817.94	876.63	same
Net Present Value Income Items					
Underwriting Income	-174	-102	-118	-80	-80
Operating Income	0	16	0	16	38
Surplus Investment Income	43	30	30	30	30
Total Income	43	46	30	46	68
Net Present Value Balance Sheet Items					
Net Operating Liabilities	1,736	1,821	1,821	1,854	1,821
Surplus	434	455	455	464	455
Net Present Value Rates of Return					
Underwriting Return (Cost of Policyholder Supplied Funds)	-10.0%	-5.6%	-6.5%	-4.3%	-4.4%
Operating Return (Risk Charge to Policyholder)	0.0%	0.9%	0.9%	0.9%	2.1%
Total Return (Shareholder Return)	10.0%	10.0%	6.5%	10.0%	14.9%

Notes: Example 3 calculates fair premium without including tax on investment income from surplus.

Example 4A is same as Example 4, except that present values are calculated without risk adjustment

Example 4 and 4A represent two alternative views. ***The financials are equivalent in both cases, but the way that risk is reflected differs***. Example 4, by introducing the risk adjustment into the discount rate, produces a ***risk-adjusted*** operating return of 0.9%, the same as in Example 2, and a ***risk-adjusted*** return to the shareholder of 10%, also the same as in Example 2. However, this is a bit circumspect since investors do not normally view the world in a risk-adjusted manner.

Example 4A determines the net present values ***without risk adjustment***. The operating return that results is 2.1% and the return to the shareholder is 14.9%. This is the return that the shareholder will actually see and it is the rate of return that will be used for comparison to alternative investments in the equity marketplace. Presenting the results in this manner provides an explicit statement of how an investor is to be compensated for the added risk involved when investing in insurance. In this example, a risk premium of 4.9% over and above the risk-free rate will be returned to the shareholder to compensate for the riskiness of making this insurance investment.

Note that the operating returns shown in Examples 4 and 4A differ by the amount of the risk adjustment. That is, the difference between 0.9% and 2.1% is the 1.3% after-tax risk adjustment (difference due to rounding).

What this shows is that the MC formulation, and NPV models generally, can be modified to produce rates of return on operations and to the shareholder, with and without risk adjustment. While the choice of whether risk adjustment is to be used is one of preference here, if reconciliation to the NCCI's IRR model is to be shown then the risk adjustment must be omitted, so that rates of return are reflected as they would appear in normal, undiscounted financials.

A more detailed discussion of the net present valued income, balance sheet, and rates of return is presented in references (3) and (4).

At this time, the NCCI and the cash flow perspective will be explored and modifications suggested for it presented.

THE IRR CASH FLOW PERSPECTIVE: REFORMULATION

The NCCI cash flow model's primary objective is to develop a series of shareholder flows, based on the underlying insurance cash flow characteristics, so that an internal rate of return (IRR) can be calculated. The IRR value thus determined represents the rate of return realized by an investor in this insurance business.

If the only concern is to develop this total shareholder return, then this result is sufficient. However, much underwriting and cash flow detail underlies this determination which can be utilized to develop other useful rate of return measures, such at the operating rate of return discussed previously. This will be explored in more detail after the specific suggested IRR model modifications are made.

The following specific modifications to the IRR model are suggested to produce additional rates of return and align its structure with the MC (revised) model.

STRUCTURAL CHANGES

Separate and clearly delineate cash flows from (1) underwriting, (2) investment of policyholder funds, and (3) investment of shareholder surplus.

1. Construct the balance sheet that corresponds to the cash flows in the model.
2. Develop IRR rate of return measures corresponding to the aggregate cash flows pertaining to underwriting and net operating income (underwriting and investment income from policyholder funds) in addition to that at the shareholder level.

PARAMETER/OPERATIONAL CHANGES

1. Solve for a fair premium based on a specified target total rate of return. Eliminate reference to such things as "profit loads" since this whole concept has little meaning in the context of total return.
2. Use a risk-free earnings rate to project investment income. If higher risk investments must be used, provide this in addition to, but not as a replacement for risk-free rates.

The NCCI usually develops a rate indication predicated on a total return, yet it still refers to a "profit load" in filings, as do many companies. This is a throwback to prior times when "profit loads" served to act as a frame of reference in the ratemaking process. With the greater role of investment income and the increased complexity of insurance contracts and cash flows, this concept should be retired. Whether intended or not, this leaves the impression that some sort of profit guarantee has been loaded into the rates. Nothing could be further from the truth. In reality, ***the profit load is simply 100% less the combined ratio, an "underwriting margin"***. This says little about profit, since it is a measure of underwriting performance only, excluding investment income, and it is on a before-tax basis. In addition, it lacks a frame of reference as to what a "fair" level ought to be in a given line of business.

Most importantly, today it generally is not a starting point in the ratemaking process. Both the Myers-Cohn and NCCI approaches deal prospectively with underwriting and investment together with their attendant risks. (Actually, Myers-Cohn as it is presently structured does not deal with investment risk, as will be discussed later.) This rate of return-oriented ratemaking basis renders the concept of profit load largely irrelevant. A so-called profit load is simply a by-product result of the process.

As an example of the type of changes suggested to the NCCI's IRR model, Exhibit V utilizes a cash flow perspective to demonstrate all flows involved in the insurance transaction for the same example used previously. The focus of Exhibit V is on the cash flow transactions that occur internally between the policyholder and company, and between the company and shareholder. Positive cash flows are ***to*** the company, negative flows are ***from*** the company. See reference (3) for more detail.

The first section of Exhibit V summarizes the transactions between the policyholder and the company and shows the total operating flows from underwriting net of premium, loss, underwriting taxes and retained earnings, before investment. In the example, in the initial time period the company receives a premium of \$877 and a tax credit of \$43. In addition, the policyholder "account" is made whole by funding the change in retained earnings in the amount of \$80 from the surplus account. The change in retained earnings captured in the policyholder level account reflects the implicit flow necessary to fully fund operational liabilities.

The net initial policyholder level cash flow is thus \$1000 at policy inception followed by payments of \$44 (change in retained earnings net of its related investment income) in years 1 and 2 and a loss payment of \$1000 at the end of year 2. The total of these flows is a net payment outflow of \$88, \$80 of which is the after-tax underwriting loss and \$8 of which is the loss of investment income on the negative retained earnings. The *IRR* ***to the policyholder*** for this stream of cash flows is 4.4%, or -4.4% ***to the company***. This is the "cost of policyholder funds" supplied to the company.

The company invests the policyholder supplied funds prior to payment of losses, and the resultant cash flows are \$65 in years 1 and 2, and total \$130.

The total operating flows including investment is \$1000 at policy inception and \$21 and -\$979, at the end of years 1 and 2, respectively. The total of \$42 is the operating income. The IRR is -2.1% ***to the policyholder***, or +2.1% ***to the company***. This is the "insurance risk charge", the rate of return implicit in the transfer of underwriting risk from the policyholder to the company. In essence, the company keeps the investment income in excess of that needed to cover underwriting costs in exchange for the transfer of risk. Viewed mathematically, the market rate of return on investments of 6.5% less the 4.4% cost of policyholder funds equals the 2.1% insurance risk charge.

EXHIBIT V

UNDERWRITING, OPERATING AND SHAREHOLDER CASH FLOWS
AND IRR'S FROM COMPANY PERSPECTIVE

	PERIOD 0	1	2	Total	NPV Not Risk Adjusted	NPV Risk Adjusted
OPERATIONS						
Premium Receipts	877	0	0	877	877	877
Loss Payments	0	0	-1,000	-1,000	-882	-904
Underwriting Tax	43	0	0	43	43	43
Ret. Earns "Funding"	80	-44	-44	-8	0	0
Total UW / PH	1,000	-44	-1,044	-88	38	16
					4.4%	**IRR**
IRR is the return on underwriting to the policyholder. This is the "Cost of Policyholder Funds" to the Company.						
Investment Income (AT)		65	65	130		
Total Operating	1,000	21	-979	42		
					-2.1%	**IRR**
IRR is the operating return to the policyholder. This is the "Risk Charge" to the Policyholder.						
SURPLUS						
Contributed	250	0	-250	0	Note (1)	
Investment Income (AT)		-16	-16	-32	Note (2)	
Oper Earnings Distribution		-21	-21	-42	Note (3)	
Net Shareholder	250	-37	-287	-74		
					14.9%	**IRR**
IRR is the total return to the shareholder.						
PERIOD RETURN						
Rate of Return on Surplus Beginning of Year		**14.9%**	**14.9%**			

Notes: (1) Governed by Constant Liability/Surplus Ratio.
(2) Distributed as Earned.
(3) Distributed in Proportion to per Period Liability Exposure.

Switching to the transactions between the company and the shareholder, three important rules govern the flow of surplus:

1. the level of surplus is controlled so that the ratio of liabilities to surplus is fixed (4 to 1 in this example),

2. investment income on surplus is returned to the shareholder as it is earned, and

3. operating earnings are distributed to the shareholder in proportion to the settlement of liability exposures over time.

These criteria will be discussed in more detail later. The net shareholder surplus flow consists of three components: the initial contribution of surplus and its subsequent withdrawal, investment income on this surplus, and operating earnings. In this example, the company received a shareholder contribution of $250 initially, followed by payments to the shareholder of $37 and $287, in years 1 and 2, respectively. This totals a net payment of $74 to the shareholder, which is the total net income. The IRR ***to the shareholder*** is 14.9% and this is the shareholder total return in this example.

An important result that is achieved when the rules governing the flow of surplus are followed in this manner is that the actual rate of return received each year by the shareholder is equal to 14.9% of each year's beginning surplus. That is to say, if dividends are paid to the shareholder using the net flows shown, the shareholder will realize a return on investment of 14.9% ***every*** year until the initial investment is fully returned.

This demonstrates how an IRR model can be utilized to provide the following three useful rates of return:

1. underwriting rate of return to the policyholder (i.e. cost of policyholder provided funds),

2. operating rate of return (i.e. insurance risk charge), and

3. total rate of return.

The NCCI model currently is structured to provide the total rate of return only. Yet the flows necessary to support the calculation of these additional rates of return can be easily extracted.

The section that follows will expand on the meaning and potential use of the operating rate of return.

OPERATING RETURN: RATE OF RETURN WITHOUT ALLOCATION OF SURPLUS

The use of total rate of return for ratemaking and profitability measurement is difficult for some to accept since this perspective involves an implicit allocation of surplus to lines of business. The *Return on Premium* (*ROP*) is often used as an alternative measure in those instances when surplus allocation is to be avoided. Unfortunately, *ROP* is lacking a contextual framework in that it has meaning only within the insurance industry. Comparable measures do not exist across other industries, and it is difficult to assess what a "fair" *ROP* is. No body of comparative reference data exists to aide in its determination in the way that cost of capital data exists to guide the selection of a target total return. Even more troublesome is the fact that *ROP's* differ widely among insurance lines of business due to differing conditions, most notably the length of the loss payout "tail" and the investment income that results. This investment income bears little direct relationship to the level of premium itself. In essence, *ROP* is a poor measure of return, since it relates income to sales, rather than to investment.

The reformulation of the Myers-Cohn NPV and IRR models produces, as a byproduct, three useful rate of return measures: (1) Underwriting Return, (2) Operating Return and (3) Total Return. Respectively, these measure the cost of policyholder supplied funds to the company, the charge to the policyholder for the transfer of underwriting risk to the company, and total return to the shareholder. The operating return is of particular interest, and it is suggested here as an alternative to the *ROP*. The operating return has the following attributes:

1. It does not require the allocation of surplus.

2. It uses the same components of income as included in the *ROP* but is a true expression of a rate of return in that operating income is measured against an "investment" rather than a sales figure.

3. Differences among lines of business are reflected automatically and, if a constant liability-to-surplus leverage factor is assumed (much like a constant premium to surplus is assumed at times when using *ROP*), the operating return is but one component of a total return approach.

4. Its definition and measurement is entirely consistent with total return.

The operating rate of return, or insurance risk charge, offers a rate of return which can be used in the establishment of a "fair" insurance return consistent (since it is mathematically part of total return) with total return as commonly accepted in the financial community. (See (3).)

The following section will briefly discuss controlling of surplus flow and recap the equivalency in rates of return for the reformulated Myers-Cohn (MCR) and NCCI models.

CONTROLLING THE FLOW OF SURPLUS AND NPV/IRR EQUIVALENCY

Surplus exists as a financial buffer in support of business writings. The amount of the initial surplus contribution and the timing of its subsequent withdrawal is an important component of total return. An IRR is calculated directly from this series of flows. From a present value perspective, the total rate of return is the total income as a percentage of the surplus committed, wherein both income and surplus are sums across the many years of financial activity as the liabilities run off.

This perspective focuses on a single policy (or accident) period and its development over future calendar periods. This differs from a calendar period view which is, in effect, constructed by summing contributions from the current and previous policy periods. It is common to view the development of calendar loss reserves in the form of a loss triangle, and if one is interested in calendar income, surplus and rate of return, it is suggested that they be viewed in an analogous manner (i.e. in the form of triangles). (See (4)).

Selecting a financial leverage factor (i.e. the ratio of liabilities to surplus) is a critical starting point since this factor determines the initial surplus contribution and the amounts of surplus subsequently released over time as liabilities are settled. The following principles guide the flow of surplus once this leverage factor has been selected (i.e. both initial shareholder surplus contribution and subsequent withdrawal):

1. The surplus level is controlled over time by a direct linkage of that level to the level of net policyholder liabilities.

2. Insurance operating earnings (underwriting and investment income on policyholder supplied funds) of each accident year are released to the shareholder (e.g. as dividends) as insurance liabilities are settled.

The release of operating earnings suggested here reflects the means by which the company (and the shareholder in turn) gains ownership to the operating profits. Operating profits result from, and are for the transfer of risk, and the release of profits in this manner corresponds to the per period exposure to this risk.

In this scenario, all three of the following will be identical:

1. the net present value ROS,

2. the internal rate of return (IRR)

3. the annual increments of shareholder earnings distribution, as a rate of each year's beginning surplus.

The balance sheet and cash flow perspectives have been used to develop the NPV and IRR rates of return, respectively. In addition, rates of return have been determined at the policyholder, company and shareholder levels. Exhibit VI provides a summary of the results and demonstrates the equivalency in returns. Properly calculated net present value (not risk adjusted) balance sheet liabilities, surplus and income produce the same underwriting, policyholder and shareholder returns as their nominal (undiscounted) counterparts do. And they are equivalent to the IRR's produced from the cash flows.

As shown in this table, the policyholder, company, and shareholder rates of return produced by the NPV and IRR approaches are identical. This important result confirms their equivalency and demonstrates that, when surplus is controlled in the same manner, the results produced by the two approaches will be equal.

This demonstration that the NPV and IRR models are equivalent given consistency in model structure and parameters has implications for ratemaking. The underlying principles, such as use of a liability / surplus leverage ratio to control surplus flow, are based on a sound rationale and are not simply academic attempts to force two models to produce the same answer. Approaches to dealing with risk, return and leverage are valid irrespective of a model's mechanics.

EXHIBIT VI

NOMINAL AND NET PRESENT VALUE RATE OF RETURN SUMMARY

NOMINAL BASIS	Year 1		Year 2	
Assets/Liabilities	Balance Sheet	Income	Balance Sheet	Income
Policyholder	1,000	-85	1,000	-3
Net Operating	1,000	-20	1,000	62
Surplus	250	16	250	16
Net	250	-4	250	79

Assets / Liabilities	Total Balance Sheet	Total Income	Total Return	IRR
Policyholder	2,000	-88	-4.4%	4.4%
Net Operating	2,000	42	2.1%	-2.1%
Surplus	500	32	6.5%	
Net	500	74	14.9%	14.9%

The reversed sign of the IRR reflects return from the policyholder perspective.

NET PRESENT VALUE BASIS

NOT RISK ADJUSTED

Assets/Liabilities	Balance Sheet	Income	Return	
Policyholder	1,821	-80	-4.4%	(1)
Net Operating	1,821	38	2.1%	(2)
Surplus	455	30	6.5%	
Net	455	68	14.9%	

(2)-(1)= 6.5% The Risk-Free Earnings Rate, After-Tax

RISK ADJUSTED

Assets/Liabilities	Balance Sheet	Income	Return	
Policyholder	1,854	-80	-4.3%	(3)
Net Operating	1,854	16	0.9%	(4)
Surplus	464	30	6.5%	
Net	464	46	10.0%	

(4)-(3) = 5.2% The Risk-Free Earnings Rate, After-Tax
Less 1.3% Risk Adjustment, After-Tax

RATEMAKING IMPLICATIONS: PARAMETER SELECTION AND KEY RELATIONSHIPS

Given a consistent set of parameters and the equivalent results produced by NPV and IRR models, it is worth exploring the question of how each model selects its key assumptions in practice. Both models require use of an investment yield, assumed here to be the risk-free rate. The risk adjustment applicable to losses is the key assumption in the Myers-Cohn model which drives the fair premium calculation. The cost of capital (i.e. the target total return) is the key assumption of the IRR model which drives the premium result of this model. As discussed earlier, if the NPV calculation of a fair premium were to be without risk adjustment then the cost of capital would be the key assumption in this model as well. This begs the question as to how the risk adjustment and cost of capital are determined and their relationship to each other.

The traditional approach is to use the Capital Asset Pricing Model (CAPM) (see (2)) as follows:

$$\text{Liability Return} = \text{Risk - Free Rate} + \text{Liability Beta} \times \text{Risk Premium}$$

(i.e. the risk adjustment equals Liability Beta x Risk Premium)

$$\text{Capital Return} = \text{Risk - Free Rate} + \text{Equity Beta} \times \text{Risk Premium}$$

Using the model structures presented and the assumptions noted previously, formulas are presented (without proof) in Exhibit VII which will be used to demonstrate the relationship among key variables. Presented are formulas for the required premium to satisfy both the NPV and IRR models simultaneously, and the formulas linking equity beta to the liability beta and vice versa.

These formulas have been used to develop Charts I through III, to demonstrate key points to be discussed momentarily. In order to produce a more realistic view, premium and expense with their respective cash flow timing assumptions will be introduced into the calculations. The previous loss liability of $1,000 has been broken into loss of $750 and expense of $250. Both premium and expense are assumed to be paid with a 3 month delay, and loss remains payable at the end of 2 years. (A quarterly model calculation has been used to develop the results to be shown). Use of loss as the sole liability and cash flow distorts the results when the risk adjustment is applied to this full amount. However, the premium and expense and associated cash flow delays have not been risk adjusted. In reality, these are subject to risk as well, but the magnitude of adjustment is likely to be much less than that pertaining to loss.

EXHIBIT VII

PREMIUM, LIABILITY BETA AND EQUITY BETA FORMULA RELATIONSHIPS

(SIMPLIFIED SINGLE PAYMENT CASE)

Premium (P) **:** Premium that is "fair" and produces IRR = Cost of Capital

$$L + L(1-D_1)\left(\frac{T R_b/F - (R - R_1)}{(1-T)(R-R_1)}\right) + E(1-D_e)\left(\frac{T R_b/F - (R)}{(1-T)(R)}\right), \text{ Assumes } N_p = 0$$

Equity Beta (B)

$$M(R_b/R_p)(K-1)(T-F+F\,T) - M\,F\,K(1-T)B_1$$

Liability Beta (B_1)

$$(R_b/R_p)\left[\frac{(K-1)(T-F+F\,T)}{F\,K(1-T)}\right] - \left[\frac{B}{M\,F\,K(1-T)}\right]$$

D_1: Loss Discount Factor with Risk Adjustment $= 1/(1+R-R_1)^N$

D: Loss Discount Factor without Risk Adjustment $= 1/(1+R)^N$

D_e: Expense Discount Factor without Risk Adjustment $= 1/(1+R)^{N_e}$

K: Risk-Adjusted PV of Loss Liabilities, Not Risk Adjusted

$$K = [(1-D_1)/(R-R_1)]/[(1-D)/(R)]$$

Note: "*L's*" in numerator and denominator cancel

M: PV of Loss Liabilities / PV of Net Liabilities, neither risk-adjusted

$$M = [L(1-D)/(R)]/[E(1-D_e)/(R)], \text{ Assumes } N_p = 0$$

CAPM Required Return on Capital $= R_b + (B)(R_p)$

CAPM Required Return on Liabilities $= R_b + (B_1)(R_p)$

P: Premium

L: Loss

E: Expense

N_p: Premium Collection Date

N: Loss Payment Date

N_e: Expense Payment Date

R_b: Interest Rate, before-tax

R: Interest Rate, after-tax

R_l: Risk Discount Adjustment, after-tax

F: Liability / Surplus Leverage Factor

T: Tax Rate

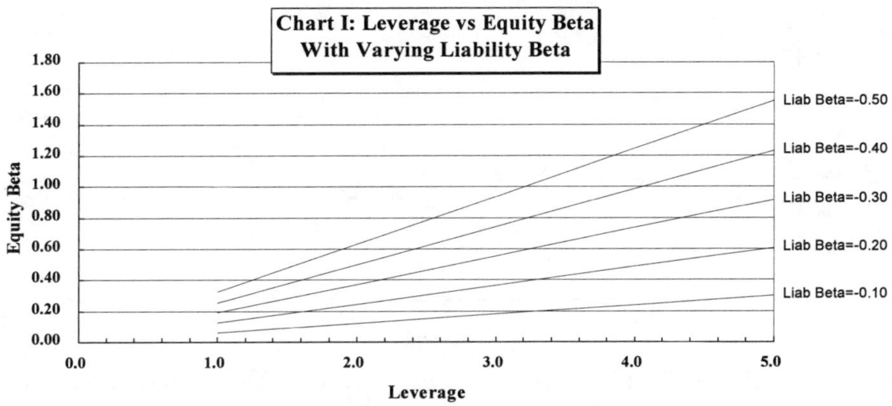

Chart I demonstrates the relationship of liability betas and equity betas, given varying levels of leverage. Chart I assumes a tax rate of 35%. As the risk adjustment of loss becomes greater, reflected in an increasingly more negative liability beta, the equity beta increases. It is interesting to note that the traditional liability beta of approximately -.20 does not produce equity betas near the 1.0 to 1.2 range observed in actual markets. The apparent discrepancy between the liability and equity betas may be explained by the following:

1. Risk adjustments are needed for ***premium and expense*** as well as losses. That is, the liability beta as presently defined understates underwriting risk.

2. The equity beta reflects the greater risk arising from investment and underwriting. Given the discrepancy between the betas, it appears that a significant portion of the equity beta is due to investment risk.

The conclusion to draw from this is that the use of a liability beta alone of -.20 will understate the fair premium required to produce a rate of return equal to the cost of capital.

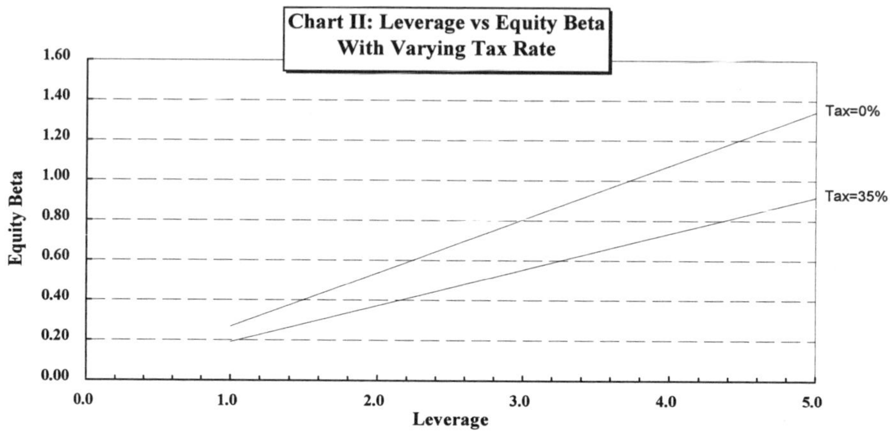

Chart II is similar to Chart I, but demonstrates how taxes affect the relationship between the betas. Chart II assumes the liability beta is -0.30. All else being equal, taxes reduce the level of equity betas. In effect, the tax acts as a suppressant to risk (i.e. volatility of return), since part of this is borne by the government.

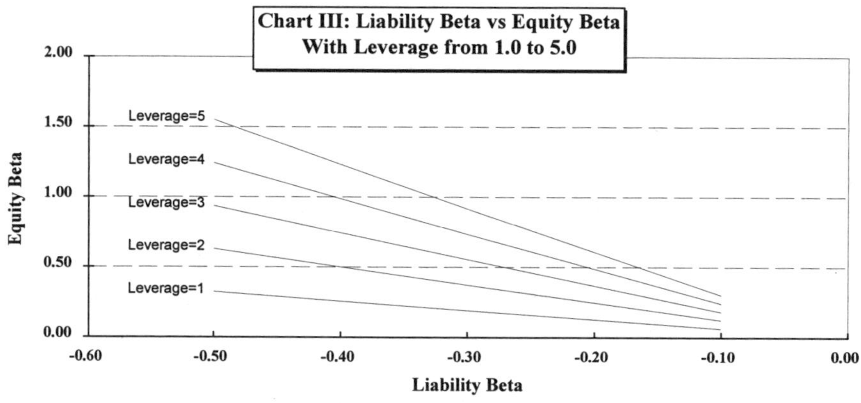

Chart III demonstrates the relationship of leverage and equity beta, given varying levels of liability betas. Chart III assumes a tax rate of 35%. From this it is easy to see how the equity beta should increase (at least in theory) as a company employs additional leverage in its operations.

It would seem intuitive that the risk inherent in liabilities, as measured here by the liability beta, is a fundamental element which should drive the resultant equity beta rather than the other way around. Unfortunately, liability betas are difficult to measure whereas equity betas can be observed much more easily in financial markets.

If a direct means can be developed to measure the risk (and in turn beta) inherent in a particular class of liabilities, then a company's mix of business and operating leverage would provide an indication of its expected equity beta. While some like to believe markets to be efficient, it is difficult to see how investors can adequately evaluate the riskiness of a particular insurance company given the complexity of insurance liabilities and the joint and interrelated risk entailed by both underwriting and investment activities. The question remains as to whether the market properly reflects risk, given the observed levels of equity betas. Perhaps the conservative, low levels of leverage at which most companies in the industry operate is the cause of lower equity beta valuations.

CONCLUSION

This article has demonstrated how conceptual and operational equivalency in net present value and IRR models can be achieved. Suggestions have been made as to how the Myers-Cohn and NCCI IRR models can be modified to permit their reconciliation. Results of the two models, the determination of "fair" premium in particular, can also be made identical given the same set of assumptions.

While many supposed ratemaking "methods" are discussed in the actuarial literature (see (10)), most of these can be shown to fall within the general umbrella of discounted cash flow models; their equivalency can be shown in much the same way as the MC and IRR models were shown in this paper.

Reconciliation of MC and IRR, and the other various "methods" as well, is more than an academic exercise. The principles brought out in this article, such as the use of liability to determine surplus levels over time, the release of operating earnings to the shareholder, and after-tax discounting, are important to the measurement of financial performance and, in turn, management decision making. Insofar as financial models are able, they contribute to the overall management of the risk / return relationship. To enhance their usefulness, it is suggested here that ratemaking approaches should have the following attributes:

1. Be supported by models which contain cash flow, balance sheet, income statement, and rate of return, and
2. Specify the principles underlying the control of all variables embodied in a total return structure, such as the flow of surplus, in addition to the "traditional" actuarial assumptions such as loss cost and trend factors.

Any approach which does not provide the full complement of financial statements of cash flow, balance sheet and income, runs the risks of error and inconsistent assumptions. Furthermore, whether stated or not, any method employed makes implicit assumptions relative to the fundamental principles which are integral to total return. Unless they are made evident, and the results measured within a total return framework, it is difficult to assess whether the results are appropriate.

Much dialogue has taken place within the insurance industry regarding the total return perspective, and its role in ratemaking and measurement of profitability. Two somewhat competing points of view remain and are represented by: (1) the actuarial ratemaking traditionalists who prefer return on premium (ROP) and (2) those with a capital market shareholder financial perspective who prefer return on equity or surplus (ROE). These two views have more to do with presentation than with substantive model development and results. The fact is that these two views are both embodied in the discounted cash flow models presented in this article. Use of either ROP or ROE as ***statistics*** is a voluntary ***choice*** and both can be used simultaneously. The results should be unaffected.

The operating rate of return presented in this article and referred to as the "risk charge" is proposed here as a measure which should be used in ratemaking rather than ROP. It is part of the total return calculation, yet it avoids the allocation of surplus to lines of business, the main concern of those who prefer ROP. (See (3) for further details.)

REFERENCES

1. Cummins, J. David, "Multi-Period Discounted Cash Flow Models in Property-Liability Insurance," Journal of Risk and Insurance, March, 1990.

2. Brealy, Richard A. and Myers, Stewart C., Principles of Corporate Finance, Fourth Edition, McGraw-Hill, Inc., 1992.

3. Bingham, Russell E., “Total Return - Policyholder, Company, and Shareholder Perspectives Principles and Applications," Casualty Actuarial Society Proceedings, 1993.

4. Bingham, Russell E., "Surplus - Concepts, Measures of Return, and its Determination," Casualty Actuarial Society Proceedings, 1993.

5. Bingham, Russell E., "Discounted Return - Measuring Profit and Setting Targets," Casualty Actuarial Society Proceedings, 1990.

6. Butsic, Robert P., "Determining the Proper Interest Rate for Loss Reserve Discounting : An Economic Approach," Evaluating Insurance Company Liabilities, Casualty Actuarial Society Discussion Paper Program, May 1988.

7. Copeland, Tom., Koller, Tim., and Murrin, Jack., Valuation - Measuring and Managing the Value of Companies, Second Edition, John Wiley & Sons, Inc., 1994.

8. Feldblum, S. "Pricing Insurance Policies: The Internal Rate of Return Model," Casualty Actuarial Society Exam Part 10 Study Material, 1992.

9. Myers, Stewart C. and Cohn, Richard A., "A Discounted Cash Flow Approach to Property-Liability Insurance Rate Regulation," Fair Rate of Return in Property-Liability Insurance, Kluwer-Nijhoff, 1987.

10. Robbin, Ira, "The Underwriting Profit Provision," Casualty Actuarial Society Exam Part 6 Study Material, 1992

11. Taylor, Greg, "Fair Premium Rating Methods and the Relations Between Them," *The Journal of Risk and Insurance*, 1994 Vol. 61, No. 4, pp. 592-615.

APPENDIX: DETERMINING ECONOMIC NET PRESENT VALUE WITH AFTER-TAX DISCOUNTING

No technical issue seems to evoke such passion as the issue of whether discounting should be on a before-tax or an after-tax basis. Both approaches have a place in the valuation process. For example, the market value of a zero coupon bond is based on a before-tax discount. The conclusion that NPV models need to use after-tax discounting is based on an understanding of two key concepts:

1. The difference between market value and economic value, and
2. the difference in corporate (or personal) taxes as they appear on an income statement and taxes as part of the time value process.

Market value, as used here, means the price the market places on a freely tradable asset (or a liability). Taxes are not accounted for at the time this exchange takes place. For example, a zero coupon bond is traded at a market value based on a discounted value determined by use of a before-tax rate. A $1,000 zero coupon bond that matures in one year will trade for $909 if interest rates are 10%. That is 1000/1.10.

If one is concerned with Economic value, however as used here, then the effect of taxes must be considered as well. Economic value is a broader concept than market value in that it encompasses both market value and the effect of taxes. For example, the $91 of income received on the same zero coupon bond will be subject to tax. If the corporate tax rate is 35%, the after-tax value will be $59. This is the economic value associated with the zero coupon bond.

The key question to ask relative to the ***economic net present value*** is "how much must be invested today to pay a $1,000 liability that is payable in one year, given that the investment income will be subject to tax?" If such a loss were funded by the purchase of a zero coupon bond for the $909 in this example, the funds available after taxes are paid would be less than $1000, since the $91 of income would be subject to tax. If this loss were funded by purchasing a zero coupon bond for $939 then exactly $1000 would remain after payment of taxes. The $939 is $1000/1.065, that is, discounted with an after-tax rate. Four examples are presented in Exhibit VIII to demonstrate this in more detail. The following observations are important to note.

1. The economic net present value of a series of cash flows must recognize that taxes will be paid on investment income essentially as it is earned.
2. The present value amount required to fund future insurance liabilities must be based on an after-tax discount rate.
3. Internal rate of return calculations are equivalent to after-tax discounting, when taxes on investment income are reflected.

As noted, the internal rate of returns produced are implicitly equivalent to after-tax discounting when taxes are reflected in the cash flows.

This economic value, with the affect of taxes included, is an integral component of net present value models. The use of after-tax discounting is necessary in order to determine the true economic net present value and to allow comparison to internal rate of return calculations. See reference (7).

The second point noted is that income taxes are not the same as the tax effect relative to the time value of money. Less confusion would exist if all taxes shown on a company's books were simply referred to as "expense", since that is what they are. These taxes have little to do with the tax treatment required in the determination of present value. Taxes, as part of the present value process to determine the time value of money, are simply reflecting the fact that the real (risk-free) earnings rate is after-tax. One sits shoulder-to-shoulder with the government, paying taxes over time as investment income is earned. It may sound a bit extreme, but the before-tax rate is essentially meaningless in terms of economic value since it is never achieved.

One last point that arises at times has to do with use of the cost of capital as a discount rate. The relevant discount rate applicable to any investment is determined by the available rate at which such an investment can be made, given similar investment options available (and properly adjusted for risk). Investors (i.e. shareholders) faced with rates of return of 15% might want to use this rate to evaluate present values to themselves. However, all funds that exist within the insurance operation, both policyholder and surplus related, face simply risk-free investment options, when risk is considered, and this should be the basis of the discount rate selection. ***Within discounted cash flow models it is NOT appropriate to discount internal cash flows at the cost of capital. This is appropriate only from a shareholder, total return perspective.*** A company can view individual lines of business as investments, each charged with producing a total return relative to a cost of capital if it chooses. However, the evaluation of present values of cash flows related to a companies assets and liabilities should be at a risk-free rate.

The challenge to the insurance company is to produce a total rate of return to the shareholder which achieves some desired cost of capital. This is separate from the determination of economic net present values within the insurance company. This article has shown that the use of risk-free, after-tax rates are appropriate to discount internal company cash flows, and further has provided the linkage to the total rate of return available to the shareholder. A shareholder is free to apply any discount rate to the net cash flows received from the company. ***Cost of capital is the appropriate discount rate only from an investor perspective.***

EXHIBIT VIII

DISCOUNTING, MARKET VALUE, ECONOMIC VALUE AND TAXES

Example 1- $1,000 Fixed Income Investment, Annual Coupon Payments

10% Yield B.T. 35.0% Tax Rate 6.5% Yield A.T.

Period	0	1	2	3	4	
Interest Earned Before Tax		100	100	100	100	
Tax		-35	-35	-35	-35	
Income After Tax		65	65	65	65	
Investment Balance	1,000	1,000	1,000	1,000	0	
						IRR
Net Cash Flow After Tax	-1,000	65	65	65	1,065	6.5%

Present Value Discounted at 10.0% = 889, at 6.5% = 1,000
IRR properly reflects rate of return on investment of 6.5% A.T
Correct Present value of 1,000 is calculated using After-Tax discount rate.

Example 2: Funding of Expected $1,000 Loss Payment at Before Tax Discount Rate

Period	0	1	2	3	4	
Interest Earned Before Tax		68	73	77	83	
Tax		-24	-25	-27	-29	
Income After Tax		44	47	50	54	
Investment Balance	683	727	775	825	0	
						IRR
Net Cash Flow After Tax	-683	0	0	0	879	6.5%

Present Value Discounted at 10.0% = 600, at 6.5% = 683
Balance of $879 falls short of Required 1,000.

Example 3: Funding of Expected $1,000 Loss Payment at After-tax Discount Rate

Period	0	1	2	3	4	
Interest Earned Before Tax		78	83	88	94	
Tax		-27	-29	-31	-33	
Income After Tax		51	54	57	61	
Investment Balance	777	828	882	939	0	
						IRR
Net Cash Flow After Tax	-777	0	0	0	1,000	6.5%

Present Value Discounted at 10.0% = 683, at 6.5% = 777

Balance of $1,000 covers loss payment due.
ECONOMIC Present Value of loss reserve must be based on After-tax Discount rate.

EXHIBIT VIII (CONTINUED)

DISCOUNTING, MARKET VALUE, ECONOMIC VALUE AND TAXES

Example 4: Zero Coupon Bond (Market value based on 10% spot rate)

Period	0	1	2	3	4	
Interest Earned Before Tax		68	75	83	91	
Tax		0	0	0	0	
Income After Tax		68	75	83	91	
Investment Balance	683	751	826	909	0	
Tax: Interest Earned Before Tax		0	0	0	0	
Tax: Income After Tax		-24	-26	-29	-32	
Tax: Income After Tax xxxx		-24	-26	-29	-32	
Tax: Investment Balance		0	0	0	0	
						IRR
Net Cash Flow After Tax	-683	-24	-26	-29	968	6.5%

Present Value Discounted at 10.0% = 596, at 6.5% = 683
MARKET Present Value of zero coupon bond is based on Before-tax Discount rate.
Value of bond will grow to $1,000 at maturity.
Value of Investment is less than $1,000 at maturity after taxes are deducted.

Conclusion: While the MARKET Value of Assets (or Liabilities) is the present value determined by BEFORE-tax discounting, their ECONOMIC value is the present value determined by AFTER-tax discounting to properly reflect the effect of taxes when assessing time value.

CHAPTER FIVE
RATE OF RETURN

By Frank D. Pierson

It's easy to say that a company prices its products to achieve at least a minimum rate of return on equity. In reality, it is not that easy. The hardest part is to allocate capital to individual contracts or lines of business; capital is not really divisible by line of business. It is available, in its entirety, to any one contract or line of business, if that contract or line produces enough losses. That being said, it is useful to think about capital as divisible, at least for pricing purposes. Since the purpose of capital is to absorb adverse deviations from expected, any method to allocate capital is acceptable so long as it differentiates among contracts or lines of business based on the risk of adverse deviation. A method that is arbitrary and does not differentiate between risks is not a viable way to allocate capital. While it might mechanically allow someone to look at rates of return on equity, it will not provide any meaningful insight as to whether a particular contract or line of business provides an attractive return for the risk taken to achieve that return.

There are many different ways to create an allocation method that differentiates based on risk. This chapter outlines one such approach in use at the author's company, a reinsurer. This approach allocates capital based on the contract's or line of business's contribution to the overall risk of the portfolio of contracts. In other words, the approach looks at the marginal capital needed to support adding new exposures to those already on the books. The capital needed is based on a risk of ruin, i.e., the company wishes to maintain its capital such that there is a constant probability that it will become insolvent as it adds exposures.

This method follows on the work of Kreps. One key difference between the approach here and that suggested by Kreps is that there is no assumption that the shapes of the distributions before and after adding the new exposures are the same. (Kreps makes this assumption implicitly by assuming that "q" is unchanged.)

INTRODUCTION

Before we discuss capital allocation among contracts for a (re)insurer, it will be helpful to discuss how an investor, in general, and an insurer, in particular, looks at investing. Once we understand the dynamics of investing, then we can develop a framework and methodology for allocating capital that is consistent with how an insurer should look at investing and analyze risk.

Within market and economic constraints, an investor will always try to maximize his/her returns. Although it may be possible to achieve a required level of return without an analysis of the risk underlying his/her investments and allocating capital accordingly, it is not possible to optimize return versus risk without such analysis.

In addition, an investor cannot maximize his/her return if part of his/her capital is uninvested because the return on actual capital is diminished by the lack of return on the amount not invested. I doubt that anyone would argue that an insurance enterprise is an investor. It is obvious that an insurer is an investor when it invests the premium funds it receives in order to pay losses. It is less obvious that an insurer is also an investor when it underwrites a new policy. An insurance policy can be viewed as a "reverse" investment made by the insurer when it agrees to write the policy. One can see that this is true if one looks at an investment in rather generic terms as either i) an outflow from the investor on which he/she expects a return or ii) the amount that the investor could lose by making the investment. Using this view, it is clear that the insurer's investment, when it writes a policy, is not the premium, but the amount of loss payments it must make, or more specifically, the amount of the shortfall between the total loss payments and the premium. Under this view, premiums (and the interest on them) become the return for making the investment.

As respects an insurer, one might argue, then, that if the total capital is not yet allocated any policy with a positive return will increase the overall return and, therefore, the insurer should write the policy. This is not the case, however, for the following reasons:

1. Investing in marginal investments (i.e., policies) today might preclude the insurer from investing in more profitable investments later, inasmuch as once it is allocated, capital may remain allocated for a significantly long time.

2. At some point, as all of the capital is allocated, the overall return approaches the average return across all investments. At that point, prior marginal investments may prevent the insurer from achieving its minimum return hurdles.

Another way of seeing writing an insurance policy as an investment is to think of the policy as an option agreement issued by the insurer. The insurer sells an option to the insured to put losses specified in the policy to the insurer. The premium is, in reality, the fee the insurer charges for giving the insured a put option.

An insurer, just as any other investor would, wants to maximize its investment returns. As an investor of the premium funds, it is fairly easy to establish whether it is maximizing its return and it can determine how much of these funds is invested at any point in time. It is much more difficult, however, for an insurer to determine how much of its capital is invested through its underwriting. Current practice in the insurance industry assumes that capital is invested proportionally with the level of premiums written by the company. Unfortunately, the rationale for this approach does not have any real theoretical basis and is, therefore, inadequate to use as a means to judge returns.

The following example illustrates how premium is unrelated to the risk assumed. Suppose that the industry standard is to allocate \$1 of capital for each \$2 of premium written. If during one year, the company wrote \$100 of premium, it would allocate \$50 of capital. If rates doubled on January 1st of the next year and the company renewed all of its annual policies on that date at the new rate level, this method would indicate that the company needed to allocate $100 of capital based on the new premium level of $200. If the company did not increase its capital to $100, it would be considered under-capitalized compared to the previous year. If risk is measured by the potential for losses to exceed premiums plus interest, the company in the later year is better capitalized than in the earlier year. Obviously, this method produces conclusions that are exactly opposite to reality.

If one accepts the concept of underwriting as investing, then financial market tools used to evaluate investment should apply equally to insurance; in fact, there has been a great deal of interest in applying such financial tools as Option Pricing Theory ("OPT") and Capital Asset Pricing Model ("CAPM") to insurance. CAPM is already in use in at least one state (Massachusetts). In addition to financial market tools, the insurance industry is trying to develop its own tools, e.g., Ruin Theory ("RT"). A few comments about the use of these methods of allocating capital or determining risk are in order (a more detailed explanation is beyond the scope of this paper).

CAPITAL ASSET PRICING MODEL

CAPM attempts to set the premium at a level that will allow a company to achieve an appropriate return in the expected case. The appropriate return, in this case, equals the risk-free rate plus a risk adjustment. The risk adjustment is dependent on "Beta" which represents the covariance of returns between the insurer and the market. CAPM asserts that an investor should be rewarded for accepting systematic risk only and not for accepting diversifiable risk, i.e., the investor is not rewarded in proportion to the risk inherent in any single investment, but is rewarded for the risk he assumes for holding a well diversified portfolio of investments. A sophisticated investor will look at a new investment by analyzing how his overall portfolio will perform with and without that investment. Only if the overall performance of his portfolio improves should the investor add that investment.

If, as discussed above, an insurer's investment is truly represented by losses, not premiums, then premiums based on current CAPM methods are not correct because they try to generate appropriate returns on premium, not loss. The basis for the analysis is inappropriate since calculating returns based on premium is equivalent to calculating returns based on the return itself rather than on the investment.

OPTION PRICING THEORY

OPT is applicable to insurance if one views an insurance contract as an option contract, i.e., the insured pays an option premium to the insurer in order to call cash to pay its losses. Obviously, the insured does not have to recover losses from the insurer. In fact, with certain loss sensitive policies there are incentives not to report losses (if losses are loaded for expenses and/or profit) once the premiums are greater than minimum levels.

What many insureds are just realizing is that there are hidden options contained in their contracts, e.g., if the insurer runs out of funds it can put the losses back to the insured. OPT attempts to calculate the equilibrium price for all of the options embedded in an insurance contract.

RUIN THEORY

European actuaries having been exploring Ruin Theory ("RT") for some time. The basic goal of RT is to calculate the minimum amount of capital required to reduce the probability of insolvency below some selected level, e.g., 1/10 of one percent, over a fixed or indefinite time horizon. RT models usually simulate the operations of the insurer over the time horizon and the initial or minimum surplus is set so that the number of iterations that result in insolvency are less than the desired level.

One can use RT to determine the level of capital needed to support a given portfolio of contracts and determine the increase in the capital required by adding an additional contract. This marginal capital can be used as the basis for allocating capital to an individual policy. For example, if writing an additional policy increases the required surplus by $1 million, then the surplus allocated to that policy is $1 million.

RT usually produces a level of surplus needed to avoid insolvency to some specified degree of confidence. Unfortunately, an insurer would be out of business long before its surplus was depleted to the point of insolvency due to the lack of confidence a low amount of surplus would generate (in theory anyway). RT must be adjusted to accommodate a different threshold.

ALLOCATED RISK CAPITAL

The rest of this chapter presents an approach to allocate capital to individual contracts in order to determine the rate of return on equity that incorporates features of CAPM, OPT and RT.

There are two levels at which the issue of capital allocation must be addressed. The first level is the allocation of capital based on market constraints. Allocation at this level is usually based on simple Surplus:Premium (*S*:*P*) or Surplus:Reserve (*S*:*R*) ratios. The amount of capital so allocated can be referred to as "Market Perception" Capital ("*MPC*"). It has been shown that the ratios used to calculate *MPC* have little or no theoretical foundations. (See above for discussion of problems of *S*:*P* ratios). The ratios are based more on tradition than on any risk analysis.

The second level of capital allocation is based on the risk of the contract being written. The amount of capital so allocated can be referred to as "Allocated Risk" Capital ("*ARC*"). In recognition of the shortcomings of using *S*:*P* or *R*:*S* ratios, the NAIC has adopted a new procedure that will calculate an insurer's *ARC* or, as the NAIC refers to it, "Risk Based" Capital ("RBC"), by applying industry ratios to various items on the balance sheet and income statement to arrive at the RBC needed as of a specific point in time. It does not include the impact of future business except to the extent that there is a risk charge for unearned premiums and written premiums (as a proxy for risk of running off the policies into the following year). One would expect that as the concept of RBC or *ARC* becomes accepted by the market place, *MPC* should approach *ARC* as old rules of thumb (P:S and R:S ratios) are no longer used. Unfortunately for our purposes, the NAIC's proposed calculation is based on the aggregate experience of the insurer rather than on the experience of an individual policy and, therefore, is not directly applicable to allocating capital to an individual policy.

The dilemma facing every investor is how best to invest all capital? Assuming an investor does not want to decrease the amount of capital he/she has to invest, one approach to investing the total capital is to allocate capital to each investment and to invest in only those investments that have returns on allocated capital greater than some minimum return. The investor maximizes his/her return by evaluating each investment opportunity individually and building a portfolio of investments, each meeting some pre-determined return. Depending on risk appetite, the investor might risk-adjust the returns before choosing the investments.

CONCEPTUAL FRAMEWORK

The distinction between *MPC* and *ARC* (and the concept of face capital developed below) gives us a framework to efficiently structure an insurer's capital, i.e., to determine an efficient mix between common equity, debt and/or preferred stock, and, at the same provide us with the means of determining the rate of return on capital at the individual policy level. Common equity usually bears the ultimate risk of any company and, in return, earns the highest yields. It is, therefore, closest in nature to the *ARC* in that the *ARC* is the amount of capital "at risk" for any given contract. Preferred stock or debt is usually used to augment yield on common equity and to supply "face" capital as needed. The excess of the *MPC* over the *ARC*, if any, could be viewed as "face" capital because it is needed only to calm outside observers and is excessive relative to the risk inherent in the book of business. Unfortunately, it is not prudent to ignore the *MPC*, at least in the long run. Market perception will dictate whether the company is viewed as strong or weak. If it is viewed as being under-capitalized, new business will not be written, or worse, only bad business will be offered to the company. In this manner, I believe that preferred stock or debt is closest in nature to the face capital.

If this characterization of capital is correct, then the proper base on which to measure return on equity ("*ROE*") is the *ARC*. Most methods in use today use *MPC* as the base on which to measure *ROE*. The cost of face capital should be included as an expense in the calculation of the *ROE* in the same way that payments on true debt or preferred stock would be included. Therefore, a charge to income would be included in the numerator rather than including the face capital in the denominator, i.e., using *MPC* as the base for the *ROE* calculation. In other words, the *ROE* should be calculated as:

$$ROE = \frac{p}{ARC} = \frac{P - L - E - r(MPC - ARC) - C}{ARC} \tag{1}$$

where p = present value profit,

P = present value of the net premium,

L = present value of the paid losses, if any,

E = present value of the expenses,

r = spread paid to borrow funds over what can earned on investing the same funds, and

C = present value of the profit commission, if any.

MPC is fairly easy to calculate. It can be based on the greater of the *S*:*P* ratio times the present value of the premium or the *S*:*R* ratio times the sum of the present value of the year-end reserves. It may be better to use year-end reserves since most analysts use the Annual Statement to evaluate financial strength. One would expect that this number should be replaced over time with the NAIC's statutory RBC calculation.

Unfortunately, *ARC* is not so easy to calculate. The proper level of *ARC* should reflect:

1. Variability in underwriting profit or loss for the contract in question, including underwriting and timing risk;

2. Interaction of that contract with all other contracts written by the company (i.e., the marginal *ARC* needed to write the additional contract);

3. Expense risk;

4. Credit risk stemming from underwriting (which may not be immaterial given the duration of our contracts);

5. Investment risk stemming from the mismatch of liabilities and assets;

6. Credit risk stemming from our investments; and

7. Off-balance sheet risk, regulatory changes, etc.

The *ARC* should also include recognition that risk exists over the entire life of a contract.

Calculating the *ARC* for all the factors listed above is theoretically complex—too complex and time consuming to be used in pricing each individual deal. The *ARC* corresponding to (4) through (7) (collectively referred to as "All Other *ARC*" or "*AO ARC*") is beyond the scope of this paper. It may be possible to include the *AO ARC* in pricing by calculating the ratio of the *AO ARC* needed for an "average" contract to some base; likely candidates are the assets, reserves or, possibly, the total *ARC* for the "average" contract.

For pricing purposes, it may not be necessary to calculate the *AO ARC* for an individual contract unless one were trying to develop an absolutely correct *ARC* for each contract. If, instead, one were trying to develop an *ARC* that can be used to determine which policies have the highest relative *ROE* and we assume that the *AO ARC* is approximately proportional to the total *ARC* for each contract, then calculating the *ARC* for (1) through (3) only (collectively referred to as "Underwriting *ARC*" or "*UW ARC*") for each contract should be sufficient. For simplicity, I will use just "*ARC*" in the rest of this paper to denote *UW ARC*.

Given the complexity of calculating the *ARC*, we need to develop a simple measure of the *ARC*. One approach would be to calculate the *ARC* in a manner similar to that used to calculate the *MPC*, i.e., apply Reserve:Surplus (*R*:*S*) ratios that vary by the amount of assumed risk. To do this, we would need to define a risk/financing continuum with very risky policies at one end (e.g., conventional cat covers) and low/no risks policies at the other (e.g., Time & Distance policies) and then subjectively assign R:S ratios to each end of the continuum and create a formula for the ratios in between (e.g., linear or log). Once the continuum is defined, the underwriter could then place each policy on the continuum and use the corresponding R:S ratio to calculate the *ARC*. One drawback of this approach is that it requires the underwriter to add another layer of assumptions on top of those used to price the deal. There is no guarantee that the placement of the policy on the continuum would be consistent with the risk implied by the distribution of profit and loss underlying the pricing. In addition, two underwriters might look at the same profit and loss distribution and place the policy in different places on the continuum.

Another approach would be to set the *ARC* equal to an amount that would guarantee that all liabilities would be honored at some specific confidence level, e.g., 90%. This approach is similar to the concept of ruin theory in that the capital is set so that the probability of insolvency or ruin is very remote. Although I use a 90% confidence level in the following examples, I believe that the right level is closer to 99% or higher (this latter level is typically used in ruin theory). The *ARC* for a single contract would be the *ARC* for the portfolio of contracts including the contract in question less the *ARC* for the portfolio without the same contract. Rodney Kreps uses a similar method to calculate a risk load for reinsurers.

There is currently much work being done, particularly in Europe, on ruin theory. Ruin theory concentrates on variability in the loss process and, therefore, it ignores some of the other risks faced by an insurance company as mentioned above, e.g., investment, credit or expense risk. To overcome that limitation, many actuaries are now attempting to simulate the entire insurance operation to incorporate the risks ignored by traditional ruin theory. Although I believe that simulating the entire insurance operation may ultimately work to estimate the total $ARC(UW\,ARC+AO\,ARC)$ for a company as a whole, I do not believe that it would work, in practice, for pricing an individual policy.

To see how this would work in practice, let's consider a few examples. Assume that for policy number 1, there is a 90% probability of a \$3,333 profit and a 10% probability of a \$10,000 loss. Using the criteria of a 90% confidence level, the *ARC* would be, therefore, equal to \$10,000. Given that the expected profit is \$2,000, the total return on *ARC* (excluding the cost of face capital, if any) would be 20%.

Assume that for policy number 2, there is a 80% probability of a \$5,000 profit and a 20% probability of a \$10,000 loss. Using the criteria of a 90% confidence level, the *ARC* would be, therefore, equal to \$10,000 (the amount closest to a 90% confidence level). Given that the expected profit is \$2,000, the return on *ARC* (excluding the cost of face capital, if any) would be 20%, the same as for policy 1.

Let's now consider the *ARC* for the two policies combined assuming that the two policies are independent. The following table will help determine the proper *ARC* given a 90% confidence level:

TABLE 1

Policy Number				
1	2	1+2	Probability	Cumulative
\$ 3,333	\$ 5,000	\$ 8,333	72%	72%
\$ (10,000)	\$ 5,000	\$ (5,000)	8%	80%
\$ 3,333	\$ (10,000)	\$ (6,667)	18%	98%
\$ (10,000)	\$ (10,000)	\$ (20,000)	2%	100%

Based on a 90% confidence level, the *ARC* would be \$6,667. As you can see, this amount is much less than the sum of the *ARC*s for each policy. In fact, the *ARC* is less than the *ARC* for either policy written separately.

This is obviously an overly simplified example, but it highlights the fact that the *ARC* of a portfolio of mutually independent policies can be significantly less than the sum of the *ARC*s for each policy assuming that each policy is expected to be profitable. In fact, the law of large numbers is another manifestation of this underlying process.

If, on the other hand, the policies were 100% positively correlated (e.g., if one of the policies above had a profit or loss, the other policy would have a profit or loss, respectively) the *ARC* would be equal to the sum of the *ARC*s of each policy. Since not all insurance policies are truly independent from each other or perfectly correlated, the correct *ARC* is somewhere between these two extremes. The *ARC* calculation can be adjusted for mutual dependence to the extent that it can be estimated and modeled.

There are a number of issues that need to be addressed before we can use this approach to calculate the *ROE* of individual contracts. Among them:

There are a number of issues that need to be addressed before we can use this approach to calculate the *ROE* of individual contracts. Among them:

I. There is a small interpretational issue involved in this method. If the aggregate *ARC* for the company after writing policy 1 in the example above is $10,000 and is $6,667 after the company writes policy 2, does this method imply that the *ARC* for both policies is equal to $3,333 or is it $10,000 for policy 1 and ($3,333) for policy 2? The latter doesn't make much sense, yet it is true that the aggregate *ARC* goes down because an additional policy was written.

   In addition, the *ARC* for each new policy can be affected by the order in which policies are added to the portfolio.

II. We need to incorporate the change in the profit/loss profile of bound deals over time. In other words, the maturing of the existing portfolio will change the probability of ruin with or without writing any additional policies. We need to reflect the existing portfolio at its current stage of maturity. This will affect pricing indirectly because as the portfolio ages, the estimate of the incremental *ARC* will vary depending on when the new policy is added to the portfolio.

III. There are accounting issues that have to be considered when selecting the ratio to be used in calculating the *MPC*. For example:

   A. should reserves that are discounted be grossed up for the discount?

   B. should reserves be gross or net of subrogation and salvage and reinsurance?

   C. should the ratio be adjusted if contracts all have contractual limits?

   D. should reserves be gross or net of an explicit risk load?

IV. This methodology does not guarantee that the aggregate *ARC* equals the company's actual capital as some people believe it should. If the aggregate *ARC* as calculated by this method were less than the actual capital, it might tell management that it could safely write new business or that it should distribute some of the capital to its shareholders. On the other hand, if the *ARC* were greater than the actual capital, it might tell management that it should cut back on its writings or it should raise more capital.

V. The choice of the confidence level is arbitrary, but it must be fairly close to 100%. There are, among others, two quite different ways to set the confidence level. The first is the more straightforward approach, i.e., management subjectively selects the level and then the aggregate *ARC* is calculated. If the aggregate *ARC* is not equal to the actual capital, then some action as outlined in (4) should occur. The second approach would be to compare the actual capital to the probabilities of various loss amounts and set the confidence level so that the aggregate *ARC* equals the actual capital. The latter approach is not as robust as the former, nor does it provide a consistent benchmark for management to assess the adequacy or efficiency of its capital.

METHODOLOGY

The method described above would be very difficult or impossible to apply at the individual policy level because of the time involved in calculating the *ARC* with and without the policy in question. It may be possible, however, to approximate this method by making some simplifying assumptions about the profit/loss distribution of the current portfolio and the new contract. To develop this approximation, let's assume:

1. That U and S^2 equal the mean and the variance, respectively, of the existing portfolio (i.e., without the new policy) and u and s^2 equal the mean and variance, respectively, of the policy for which we wish to calculate the return on equity.

2. That the *ARC* for the existing portfolio will be defined as an amount such that the probability that an aggregate loss is less than or equal to that amount is equal close to 100%. If we set the ARC_e so defined, equal to $q_1 S - U$, we can calculate q_1 as:

   $q_1 = \left(ARC_e + U\right)/S$, where ARC_e is the value at the selected confidence level.

3. That the mean of the new portfolio (i.e., including the new policy) would be equal to $U + u$ and that the standard deviation would be equal to $\left(S^2 + s^2 + 2cSs\right)^{\frac{1}{2}}$, where c is the correlation coefficient between the new policy and the existing portfolio. Let's denote $\left(S^2 + s^2 + 2cSs\right)^{\frac{1}{2}}$ by S_2.

Based on these assumptions, the ARC_n for the new portfolio is equal to:

$$
\begin{aligned}
ARC_n &= q_2\left(S^2 + s^2 + 2cSs\right)^{\frac{1}{2}} - (U + u) \\
&= q_2 S_2 - (U + u)
\end{aligned}
$$

where q_2 is calculated in a manner similar to q_1.

If we define, as suggested above, the *ARC* for the new policy as the difference between the *ARC* for the existing and new portfolios, then the *ARC* for the new policy would be equal to:

$$ARC_p = ARC_n - ARC_e = q_2 S_2 - q_1 S - u\,,$$

or

$$ARC_p = q_1\left(S_2 - S\right) - u + \left(q_2 - q_1\right)S_2\,,$$

where

$$\left(S_2 - S\right) = \left(S^2 + s^2 + 2cSs\right)^{\frac{1}{2}} - S\,.$$

If we multiply the right hand of the formula for $\left(S_2 - S\right)$ by one in the form of $\left(s/s\right)$, we get

$$\begin{aligned}\left(S_2 - S\right) &= \left(s/s\right)\left(S^2 + s^2 + 2cSc\right)^{\frac{1}{2}} - S\left(s/s\right)\\ &= s\left(\left(S/s\right)^2 + \left(s/s\right)^2 + 2cSs/s^2\right)^{\frac{1}{2}} - S\left(s/s\right)\\ &= s\left(\left(S/s\right)^2 + 1.0 + 2c\left(S/s\right)\right)^{\frac{1}{2}} - \left(S/s\right)s.\end{aligned}$$

The term $\left(S/s\right)$ reflects the size of the variability in the existing portfolio relative to the volatility of the new policy. As this term gets larger, the value of $\left(S_2 - S\right)$ approaches the value of c. Therefore, if we assume that the term $\left(S/s\right)$ is sufficiently "large," it can be shown that:

$$\left(S_2 - S\right) = cs,\ c \neq 0\,.$$

and the formula for *ARC* (from now on, the subscript "*p*" is dropped to keep the rotation cleaner) reduces to:

$$ARC = q_1 cs - u + \left(q_2 - q_1\right)S_2\,,$$

or

$$ARC = q_1 cs - u + K\,,$$

where $K = \left(q_2 - q_1\right)S_2$. K can be regarded as "portfolio adjustment factor."

This formula for ARC has a straightforward interpretation. For any new contract, the Allocated Risk Capital is equal to the maximum loss that the company will tolerate at a specified confidence level (represented by the term q_1cs and based on the volatility of the new contract) less the expected profit of an average contract (represented by the term *u*, assuming that all contracts are the same size) less an adjustment factor to reflect the fact that the contract will be written in the context of an existing portfolio (represented by the term *K*).

It should be noted that *q* so determined is at the portfolio level, not at the individual policy level. In other words, the value of $qs - u$ at the individual policy level may not correspond to a 99% confidence level. In fact, it may correspond to a level significantly less than that.

ANNUALIZING THE RETURN ON ARC

Now that we have a workable formula to calculate the *ARC* for an individual policy at inception of the policy, let's return to our formula for *ROE*, i.e., $ROE = p/ARC$. This *ROE* calculation does not reflect the fact that the *ARC* allocated to support the policy remains committed throughout the life of the policy as measured by the presence of risk. It would be great if the underwriter knew immediately after binding the policy whether it made or lost money. Unfortunately, the underwriter does not know the final outcome of a deal for many years after he/she writes it (an extreme example of this are all the insurers who wrote GL policies in the 40's who are now paying out massive amounts for asbestosis and pollution claims). Until we are certain about the outcome of a policy, the market will require a company to support it with equity or *ARC*. Obviously, the level of *ARC* does not stay constant over time because we learn incrementally about the results of a policy and risk is amortized away. *ARC* typically starts out at its maximum value (and it may stay at that level for some time) and then decreases over time, finally reaching zero when all uncertainty about the policy is extinguished. How can we determine how long *ARC* is committed to any policy?

To understand how long the *ARC* is committed to a policy, it is necessary to understand the source of the risks underlying the policy. Some of sources of the risk underlying insurance policies (due to uncertainty about these items) are:

- Subject premium volume
- Subject exposure volume (which may be different from premium)
- Ultimate loss levels
- Timing of premium and loss payments
- Catastrophe losses
- Mix of business/classes
- Mix by territory

Inuring reinsurance

Lack of actual data/immature of most recent historical data

Rate changes/Inflation

Risk amortizes away as the uncertainty about these items is reduced.

Uncertainty about the above items is eliminated over two different, overlapping time periods: the exposure period and the period over which the losses pay out. The first period generates Exposure Risk and the second one generates the Loss Risk. Exposure Risk covers most of the items listed above. I believe that this risk has a relatively very short life. For some lines of business, for example, property, this risk is near zero shortly after the policy expires. For other lines of business, for example, workers compensation, this risk is near zero by 12-24 months after the end of the policy period. If that is true, then this risk amortizes over the life of the policy plus 12-24 months, less in the first part of the policy period and more quickly later.

Loss Risk stems from uncertainty of the ultimate losses and their payment pattern. This risk is well known to actuaries as they try to set reserves each year. This risk amortizes over time as losses are paid and is zero when all losses have been settled. It is not clear whether this risk amortizes pro-rata or faster than the reserve run-off pattern. It is fairly easy to produce cases where this risk amortizes quicker than the reserve run-off pattern. I believe that it is conservative to assume is that this risk amortizes pro-rata as reserves run-off.

Unfortunately, the relative influence on the total risk of a policy is not constant for all classes of business. For example, much of the risk for a stop-loss on an auto liability book would expire within 12-24 months after the end of the policy period even if the ceded losses would not be paid for a number of years after that since the ultimate losses and the payment pattern should be well established at that time. For excess D&O or other long-tail lines, the bulk of the risk would remain outstanding for a much longer time.

We could factor in the influence of different classes of business by changing the weights given to the two patterns. Figure 1 shows how this might work. The Exposure Risk is assumed to run-off evenly over a three year period. The Loss Risk follows the loss reserve run-off (assumed to be zero for seven years and then 20% per year thereafter). The graph also shows weighted averages giving 80% and 50% to the Exposure Risk.

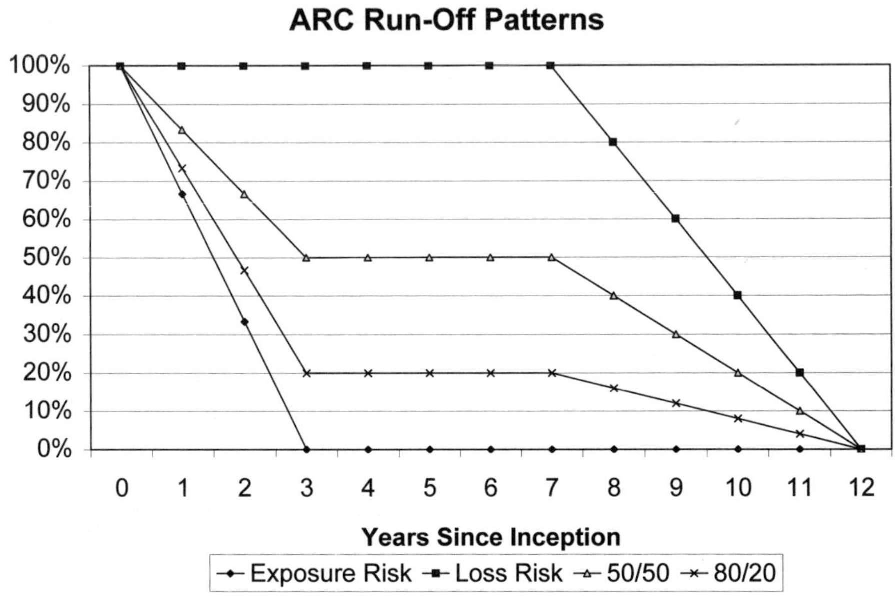

Now that we have a method to determine the *ARC* and the speed at which it amortizes, it is now possible to determine the return on the insurer's "investment" when it writes a policy. If we assume that the insurer "invests" an amount equal to the *ARC* in each new policy, we can then calculate the internal rate of return ("*IRR*") of the policy, i.e., the rate that equalizes the present value of the investment and the present value of the return that the investor receives for writing the deal. The return the "investor" receives is equal to the initial investment plus the profits which the investor receives over time. We assume that the initial investment is returned to the investor as the risk amortizes away. We assume that the investor receives the expected profits as they would be recognized in the insurer's financials.

An example may be helpful. Let's assume that the *ARC*, calculated as described above, is \$100 and that we expect the *ARC* needed at the end of years one through four is \$100, \$81, \$25 and \$0, respectively. Let's further assume that the profit of \$10 is recognized evenly in the first two years. The flows underlying this investment are, therefore:

TABLE 2

Year	ARC	ARC Flow	Profit Flow	Total Flow
0	$ 100	$ (100)	--	$ (100)
1	$ 100	$ 0	$ 5	$ 5
2	$ 81	$ 19	$ 5	$ 24
3	$ 25	$ 56	$ 0	$ 56
4	$ 0	$ 25	$ 0	$ 25

The *IRR* of the last column is approximately 5%.

REMAINING ISSUES

There are a number of issues that still need to be discussed or addressed:

1. There is nothing to prevent the *ARC* produced by the above formula from being negative. If the *ARC* is negative, the new policy is a net provider of capital rather than a consumer of capital. In this particular case, the company should always write these deals because as net equity providers these are an extremely cheap form of capital.

2. There is nothing to prevent the face capital from being negative. In other words, when face capital is negative, the policy will be a net provider of face capital. This only happens when $ARC > MPC$. These contracts help to reduce the need for face capital across the entire portfolio. In essence, other deals "borrow" this face capital and, therefore, a deal with negative face capital should be credited with the investment income it "earns" by loaning its face capital to other deals.

3. The above formula for *ARC* does not reflect parameter risk and unquantifiable extra contractual risks and a separate loading should be included in the *ARC* calculation. The question that naturally arises is how to add a load for parameter risk (if we could quantify it, it would no longer be parameter risk) or for extra-contractual risk (if we could quantify or identify it, we could eliminate it). There are a number of candidates that could serve as a basis for this loading, among them:

    Reinsurance Premium

    ARC

    MPC

    Limit

    Limit - Premium

And I am sure that there are others. My recommendation is the aggregate limit less the maximum premium. This value represents the maximum exposure (excluding the risk that the limit provision of the contract is not upheld). The above formula for *ARC* could be modified to include such a loading as follows:

$$ARC = qcs - u + w + K$$

where $w = 1\%(\text{limit} - \text{premium})$. The w value could be referred to as the "who knows factor."

4. At what level within a company should the value of q be determined? Should there be a single value of q for the entire company, by line of business or territory or some other market segment? I believe that the value of q should be set at the overall company level unless capital has been allocated down to line of business, etc. and the company wishes to allocate capital among policies at this lower level at different confidence levels.

5. The choice of q is dependent on the confidence level required by management and should reflect management's risk tolerance. But even after management has selected the confidence level, should the portfolio and the new policy be judged on an ongoing concern basis or in a run-off situation (the unearned portion of policies written are canceled)?

In any case, the value of q must be based on the existing portfolio including the policies that were written in the past and are in run-off. In other words, the value of q depends on more than just the current policy or accident year. As such, as the book matures it will affect the shape of the profit/loss distribution.

CHAPTER SIX
INVESTMENT-EQUIVALENT REINSURANCE PRICING

By Rodney Kreps, FCAS, MAAA, PhD

SUMMARY

Reinsurance pricing is usually described as market-driven. In order to have a more theoretical (and practical) basis for pricing, some description of the economic origin of reinsurance risk load needs to be given. A special-case algorithm is presented here which allows any investment criteria of return and risk to be applied to a combination of the reinsurance contract and financial techniques. The inputs are the investment criteria, the loss distributions, and a criterion describing a reinsurer's underwriting conservatism. The outputs are the risk load and the time-zero assets allocated to the contract **when it is priced as a stand-alone deal**. Since most reinsurers already have a book of business and hence contracts mutually support each other, the risk load here can be regarded as a reasonable maximum. The algorithm predicts the existence of minimum premiums for rare event contracts, and generally suggests reduction in risk load for pooling across contracts and/or years. Three major applications are (1) pricing individual contracts, (2) packaging a reinsurance contract with financial techniques to create an investment vehicle, and (3) providing a tool for whole book management using risk and return to relate investment capital, underwriting, and pricing.

I. INTRODUCTION

There has been an evolution over the last few years toward looking at an insurance or reinsurance enterprise as a whole, rather than seeing underwriting, investments, dividend policy, and so forth as a set of disjoint pieces. Whereas in modern financial theory various approaches to the interaction of risk and reward are reasonably well developed, for reinsurance in particular the very measurement of risk has been (and arguably still is) more of an art than a science. It is generally agreed that surplus creates capacity and writing business uses up surplus—but there is no agreement on how that happens.

This paper proposes a possible model for the special case where the contract is priced on a stand-alone basis, i.e., it is the reinsurer's only business. The risk loads (and hence pricing) derived here are maximal because reinsurers generally have an ongoing book of business. This book is mutually supporting, in that usually not all of it goes bad at the same time. Pricing on a stand-alone basis is equivalent to assuming that the whole book is fully correlated. In some sense, stand-alone pricing will in general result in larger risk loads than are actually needed.

Although the give and take of the market will in the end determine what prices are actually charged for contracts, both insurer and reinsurer can use an economic pricing model to help decide whether to write the contract, since for the insurer the decision not to reinsure externally is the decision to self-reinsure. The intent of this paper is to present a paradigm that will allow the combination of a reinsurance arrangement and suitable financial techniques to be thought of as an investment alternative. This allows a firm's investment criteria to be applied.

What will actually be done is to assume investment criteria in the form of a target mean return and risk measure thereon, and to obtain from the paradigm the necessary risk load and putatively allocated assets for the reinsurance arrangement.

The paradigm is as follows: when the reinsurer accepts a contract, it arranges to have available at every time of loss sufficient liquifiable assets to cover possible losses up to some safety level. These assets arise from premium and assets allocated from surplus, both of which are invested in appropriate financial instruments. The reinsurer wishes to have at least as favorable return and risk over the period of the contract as it would when doing its target investment with the underlying allocated assets.

Note that this is not—at least to the author's knowledge—how reinsurers currently do their pricing, nor is it advocated (except in special circumstances) as an operating procedure for reinsurers. It is meant as a way of deriving risk loads by relating them to investment criteria. At the same time, it is grounded in notions which make intuitive sense. Certainly in the real world reinsurers had better plan to have assets available to pay losses; otherwise they are planning for bankruptcy. **This paradigm essentially looks at risk load as an opportunity cost and represents it as a (partially offset) cost of liquidity**. This is not to say that this is the only way of looking at risk loads—but it is a simple and intuitive one.

The **loss safety level** is essentially a measure of reinsurer company conservatism. Again, it is intuitive that some measure of company conservatism must be present in a risk load paradigm. The more conservative the company, the higher the safety level and the less probable it is that the safety level will be exceeded. Higher safety levels will typically result in more expensive contracts.

A mundane example of a safety level occurs when a person decides to build a house in snow country. The question is, how strong to build the roof for snow load? If it is a cabin for only a few years, perhaps building to survive the 10 year storm will be enough. If it is meant for the grandchildren, perhaps the 200 year storm is more appropriate. It is, of course, more expensive to build it stronger. In any case some level is chosen depending on the builder's criteria.

The safety level used in the examples here will be the amount of loss associated with a previously chosen probability, such as the 99.9% level, i.e., the loss associated with a one thousand year return time. In some circumstances (see Section II.3) the full amount of the contract may be the appropriate safety level. There are, of course, other possibilities than a probability level. One such would be to choose a safety level of loss high enough such that the average value of the excess loss over that level is an acceptably small fraction of the mean loss. Another is that the average excess over the safety level times the probability of hitting the safety level is below some value. Whereas it would be interesting to examine various choices in the context of different management styles, for the present purposes the essential remark is that any quantifiable measure can be used.

Clearly, a risk load paradigm must involve the cost of capital—and more specifically measures of **investment return and risk** for comparison to the capital markets. A *reductio ad absurdum* shows the argument: if capital were free and freely available, insurance, much less reinsurance, would be unnecessary since a firm in temporary trouble would simply borrow to overcome difficulties. The measure of investment risk used here will be the standard deviation (or variance). Equally possible would be to use one of the more sophisticated strictly downside measures, such as a semi-variance or the average value of the (negative) excess of return below some trigger point such as the risk-free rate. Especially in the cases here where very large losses may generate negative results, such a downside risk measure may be desirable. These measures do not give pretty formulae, but are easily used numerically. Again, any quantifiable measure is feasible.

There are two types of **financial techniques** that will be considered. Please note that other techniques are possible; these are just two of the simplest. The first is where the reinsurer takes the capital that it would have put into the target investment (which could be, for example, corporate bonds), and puts it into a risk-free instrument such as government securities. This will be referred to as a **swap**. Even though such terminology is not technically correct, it carries the right flavor. The cost associated with this is basically the loss of investment income, but there is also a gain in that risk is reduced.

This technique will result in simple formulae[1], but in various examples it often turns out to create a higher risk load, and hence to be more expensive (to the cedent) and therefore less competitive than the second type of technique: buying **"put" options**. These options are the right to sell the underlying target investment at a predetermined strike price at maturity (we only consider European options). Here the strike price will be what investment in risk-free securities would have brought, so that the reinsurer is buying the right to sell the target investment at a return not less than the risk-free rate.

The Black-Scholes[2] formula is used to price the option. The distribution of investment returns underlying this formula is assumed for the reinsurer's target investment. The cost of these options will contribute to the risk load, but this is partly offset because the options both increase the return and decrease the variance of the target investment.

This treatment will not include the effects of reinsurer expenses, nor of taxes. However these could be put in, especially in the simulation models described in the latter part of

[1]For the variance measure of investment risk. As remarked earlier, other measures will in general not give simple formulae.

[2]See the discussion of Black-Scholes in, e.g., the CAS Part 5 reading, "Principles of Corporate Finance - 4th Edition" by Brealey and Myers (McGraw-Hill, 1991) page 502 ff..

the paper. For the taxes, one would have to make some assumptions as to whether the contract would affect any possible Alternative Minimum Tax situation. Probably this could best be treated by looking at the reinsurer's whole underwriting book and investment structure with and without the contract of interest. This is a can of worms which the author prefers not to open in this paper.

In Section II, the paper will first discuss the case of a single loss payment at the end of one year. In Section II.1, the swap is treated and in Section II.2, the option. These simple discussions will illustrate the general principles, so that they will hopefully not be obfuscated by the details of the subsequent development. For readability of the paper, technical details are relegated to appendices. In Section II.3 the limiting case of a high excess layer is presented, where it is shown that a minimum premium results. This is in accord with actual market behavior. In Section III the single payment case is extended to arbitrary known time of loss. Section III.1 is a numerical example, and Section III.2 is some general remarks on pooling and other subjects. The principal remark here is that whereas this paradigm may be used in the pricing, it is probably not either necessary or desirable that the reinsurer actually carry out the actions modeled by the paradigm for an individual contract.

The multiple payment case is illustrated in Section IV with a spreadsheet example. In this case, there are no longer simple formulae available, and simulation modeling must be explicitly used. Section IV.1 discusses the extension of the loss safety constraint. Section IV.2 describes the spreadsheet at average values—the analog of taking the mean of the stochastic equation, as was done in Section II. Section IV.3 gives an example and discussion of a full stochastic run. Section IV.4 has various comments on the spreadsheet. Section V contains some general remarks, principal among which is that the risk loads considered here are extreme: actual book pricing should be less.

II. SINGLE PAYMENT AT ONE YEAR

The principal determinants of interest here are

s = the dollar safety level associated with the loss distribution.
L = the amount of the loss.
μ_L = the mean value of the loss.
σ_L = the standard deviation of the loss.
r_f = the risk-free rate.
y = the yield rate of the target investment.
σ_y = the standard deviation of the investment yield rate.
P = the premium net to the reinsurer after expenses.

Quantities derived from the above are

A = the assets allocated by the reinsurer.
F = the funds initially invested: premium and assets less option cost, if applicable.
R = the risk load in the premium: the premium less the discounted expected loss.

The premium in all cases is the risk load plus the expected loss discounted at the risk-free rate. Note that this premium does not include any reinsurer expenses. For a single payment at one year,

(1) $$P = R + \frac{\mu_L}{1+r_f}$$

The constraints of the paradigm may now be stated as (1) the investment result from F as input must be at least s, and (2) the standard deviation of the overall result must be no larger than σ_y.

Although the fundamental cash flow relations are stochastic, it is possible in this section to obtain explicit formulae for the mean and variances involved, and hence get explicit forms for the risk load. In Section IV, the mean is easily obtained, but the variance of the final result of the fundamental cash flow will have to be determined by simulation.

II.1 SWAP CASE

At time zero the reinsurer has an inflow of P and an outflow of

(2) $$F = (P + A).$$

Since the investment is in risk-free securities, at the end of the year the reinsurer has an inflow of $(1+r_f)F$ and an outflow of the loss L. The internal rate of return (*IRR*) on these cash flows is defined by the fundamental stochastic relation

(3) $$(1 + IRR)A = (1 + r_f)F - L$$

where both L and *IRR* are stochastic variables. Taking the mean value of this equation and asking that the mean value of the *IRR* be the yield rate y gives

(4) $$(1 + y)A = (1 + r_f)F - \mu_L$$

which may be expressed as[3]

(5) $$R = \frac{(y - r_f)}{(1 + r_f)} A.$$

[3]For readability, derivations of more than one line are done in Appendix 3.

Another equation is needed to solve the system, and there are two other constraints that must be satisfied, a loss safety constraint and an investment variance constraint. In general, it is clear that by making the asset base large enough the fractional variability of results can be made as small as desired and the funds available as large as desired. Hence there is always a solution. Both constraints may be phrased as placing lower limits on the allocated assets, so satisfying the more restrictive will satisfy both.

For the safety constraint, requiring the funds available at the year end to be greater than or equal to the safety level gives

(6) $$(1+r_f)F \geq s\,.$$

Combining Eqs. (4) and (6) to eliminate F

(7) $$A \geq \frac{(s-\mu_L)}{1+y}$$

and consequently from Eqs. (5) and (7) the risk load at the equality is

(8) $$R = \frac{(y-r_f)(s-\mu_L)}{(1+r_f)(1+y)}$$

and from Eq. (1) the premium before expenses is

(9) $$P = R + \frac{\mu_L}{1+r_f}\,.$$

This is the result for the safety constraint.

For the variance constraint, since there is no variability in the investment return (because it is risk-free) the standard deviation of the *IRR* is given from Eq. (3) as

(10) $$A\sigma_{IRR} = \sigma_L\,.$$

The investment constraint is that the *IRR* should have variance less than or equal to that of the target investment, which gives

(11) $$A \geq \sigma_L / \sigma_y$$

and using Eq. (5) again

(12)
$$R = \frac{(y - r_f)}{(1 + r_f)} (\sigma_L / \sigma_y) .$$

Given typical values for the loss distribution and the target investment, the latter is likely to be the more stringent constraint. This will be true when

(13)
$$(s - \mu_L) / \sigma_L < (1 + y) / \sigma_y .$$

For a one in a thousand safety level and a normal distribution, the number on the left is around 3. For more positively skewed distributions, it will be larger; but in the work of the author it is seldom as large as 5 for typical reinsurance layers. However, in the example used later of an unlimited cover on a lognormal with coefficient of variation 2, the ratio on the left is over 10. The unlimited cover is a mathematical convenience for illustration rather a realistic contract, at least since pollution losses became noticeable. Plausible values for the ratio on the right are easily up around 12 for bonds and higher than 5 for equities.

II.2 OPTION CASE

At time zero the reinsurer will receive the premium, but keep the initial assets invested in the target investment. It will also buy an option to sell the target investment at the end of the year for the value that the risk-free technique would have achieved. By doing so it has obtained an instrument that eliminates that portion of the investment return distribution which lies below the risk-free rate. This will have the effect both of increasing the mean return from the investment and decreasing its standard deviation.

Let

- r = the rate (cost per dollar of investment protected) of a put option.
- I = investment return
- i = mean investment return (determined in Appendix 2).

The value of r depends upon the underlying investment parameter σ, which is determined by y and σ_y and defined in Appendix 1. For small values of the ratio of σ_y to $(1+y)$, it is approximately true that

(14)
$$\sigma = \frac{\sigma_y}{(1 + y)}$$

and

(15)
$$r = \frac{1}{\sqrt{2\pi}} \sigma \left(1 - \frac{\sigma^2}{24} \right) .$$

However, the examples below use the exact formula from Appendix 1. At time zero the reinsurer has an inflow of P and an outflow of $(P+A)$. However, the funds available for investment have decreased by the cost of the option. Specifically, Eq. (2) becomes

$$F = P + A - rF \tag{16}$$

so

$$F = \frac{(P+A)}{(1+r)}. \tag{17}$$

Since the investment is now in risky securities (hedged at the bottom end to not drop below the risk-free rate), at the end of the year the reinsurer has an inflow of $(1+I)F$ and an outflow of the loss, L. The internal rate of return on these cash flows is defined by a fundamental stochastic relation similar to Eq. (3):

$$(1+IRR)A = (1+I)F - L. \tag{18}$$

Again, requiring that the mean value of IRR be the target yield rate gives

$$(1+y)A = (1+i)F - \mu_L. \tag{19}$$

This does not simplify easily, but fundamentally we have two unknowns—R and A—and this is one equation relating them. The other equation will come from whichever is the more restrictive constraint, as before.

The loss safety constraint on the funds available is again

$$(1+r_f)F \geq s. \tag{6}$$

It should be noted that the actual funds available are likely to be larger than this, since r_f represents the <u>minimum</u> value of the realizable investment return, thanks to the option. Combining Eqs. (6) and (19) to eliminate F, the allocated assets are

$$A \geq \frac{1}{1+y}\left\{\frac{(1+i)}{(1+r_f)}s - \mu_L\right\}. \tag{20}$$

This is larger than in the swap case since $i > y > r_f$.

The expression for the risk load at equality is[4]

(21) $$R = \frac{1}{(1+r_f)(1+y)}\left[s\{(1+y)(1+r)-(1+i)\} - \mu_L(y-r_f)\right].$$

For $i = r_f$ and $r = 0$ the results of the previous section are, of course, obtained in the above two formulae.

In order to express the investment variance constraint it is necessary to decide the correlation between the loss and the investment return. The linkage by inflation suggests that there may be a negative correlation—if inflation rises, typically claims costs rise and bond values fall. In the interest of simplicity the assumption will be made that the correlation is zero, although there is no essential complication induced by taking a non-zero value. The standard deviation of the investment return is derived in Appendix 2 and written as σ_i. When the variance of the *IRR* is required to be that of the target investment, there results

(22) $$(A\sigma_y)^2 = (F\sigma_i)^2 + (\sigma_L)^2 .$$

The value of the initial fund F from the equation for the mean may be substituted into this, resulting[5] in a quadratic equation for A of the form

(23) $$-aA^2 + 2bA + c = 0$$

with

(24) $$a = \sigma_y^2(1+i)^2 - \sigma_i^2(1+y)^2$$

(25) $$b = L(1+y)\sigma_i^2$$

(26) $$c = L^2\sigma_i^2 + \sigma_L^2(1+i)^2 .$$

All three coefficients are positive, the last two because of their explicit construction and the first because the option both decreases the variance and increases the mean of the investment return compared to the target values.

The positive solution is

[4]See Appendix 3.

[5]See Appendix 3. The forms corresponding to a non-zero correlation are also given there.

(27) $$A = \frac{b + \sqrt{b^2 + ac}}{a}$$

and[6]

(28) $$R = A\frac{(1+r)(1+y)-(1+i)}{1+i} + L\left[\frac{1+r}{1+i} - \frac{1}{1+r_f}\right].$$

In the limit as $\sigma_i \to 0$ the solution for A goes back to the ratio of standard deviations; with $i = r_f$ and $r = 0$ the risk load returns to the earlier form found in the swap case, as it should.

II.3 HIGH EXCESS LAYER AND MINIMUM PREMIUM

An interesting application of these formulae is in the case of a high excess layer or any similar finite rare event cover. A non-zero rate on line (ratio of premium to limit) is predicted even for cases where the loss probability goes to zero.

For simplicity, take the loss distribution to be binomial: There is a probability, p, of hitting the layer, and if it does get hit it is a total loss. The safety level, s, is taken to be the limit (total amount payable) of the layer. Note that the 99.9% level is not an appropriate way to get the safety level (especially for $p < 0.001$), but there is still in fact an intuitive value.

The mean loss μ_L is ps and the variance of the loss is $p(1-p)s^2$. As the probability p gets smaller, corresponding to higher and higher layers, in both the swap and option cases the variance constraint gives A and R both going to zero as $\sqrt{p}$. However, the safety constraint in both cases is linear in p with a non-zero intercept. In the option case, the rate on line[7] *(ROL)* in the limit as p goes to zero is

(29) $$ROL = \frac{(1+y)(1+r)-(1+i)}{(1+r_f)(1+y)}.$$

This is obtained by setting $L = 0$ in Eq. (21) and recognizing ROL as the ratio of R to S.

As usual, the swap version may be obtained by letting $r = 0$ and $i = r_f$, which results in

[6] See Appendix 3.

[7] That is, the ratio of premium to limit.

$$ROL = \frac{1}{1+r_f} - \frac{1}{1+y} = \frac{y-f}{(1+r_f)(1+y)}. \tag{30}$$

The latter form suggests that the minimum ROL is of the order of the real target return—i.e. the excess of the return over the risk-free rate. However, often the option from Eq. (29) will produce a smaller number. For the investment values such as are used below it is typically on the order of half as large. As the investment standard deviation gets small the swap ROL stays the same (of course) and the option ROL gets small because the option cost gets small and the mean investment return approaches the target yield. It is important to remember that this is all in the limit where the $p = 0$, so that the variance constraint is always satisfied. For small but currently reinsured probabilities—say in the range from 1% to 0.1%—as the target standard deviation of investment is made small the variance constraint will eventually become dominant.

In the market, a minimum rate on line is generally justified by underwriters as a charge for using surplus. This approach is consistent with that view, and also allows quantification of the charge.

III SINGLE PAYMENT AT ARBITRARY TIME

If all the returns in the preceding are interpreted as total return up to time t, then the formulae hold without modification. When we wish to express the returns in terms of the equivalent annualized returns, the results hold after the following replacements are made:

$$(1+i) \to (1+i)^t \tag{31}$$

$$(1+y) \to (1+y)^t \tag{32}$$

$$(1+r_f) \to (1+r_f)^t \tag{33}$$

The forms for the option rate and the standard deviations given in Appendix 2 contain the time dependence.

III.1 NUMERICAL EXAMPLE

For any one-payment situation, the recommended procedure is as follows:

1. Calculate the four risk loads and allocated assets - safety and variance constraints for the option and swap cases.
2. Find for each financial technique which constraint has the larger allocated assets—this is the dominant one.

3. Compare the dominant risk loads for different techniques and choose the smaller—this is the preferred[8] solution.

This whole calculation is easily put on a spreadsheet. For the specific example, the following annualized values have been taken: yield rate y = 5.3%; standard deviation of the yield rate σ_y = 8.4%; risk-free rate r_f = 3.6%. The loss distribution is taken lognormal with mean of $1M (million) and a standard deviation of $2M. The safety level of loss is taken as the 99.9% level, $22,548,702. Parenthetically, for a one-year interval this makes the left-hand side of Eq. (13) 10.8, while the right-hand side is 12.5, suggesting that variance will be the dominant constraint for the swap. For a two-year interval, the right-hand side changes to 8.9 and safety is dominant in the swap. The large value of the left-hand side is due to the fact that this is an unlimited contract.

As an example of the recommended procedure, the following results can be derived from the formulae in the preceding sections for a time of two years, and are incorporated in Table 1 below:

	SWAP		OPTION	
constraint	variance	safety	variance	safety
assets	$15,963,111	$19,434,097	$23,024,033	$20,737,421
risk load	$528,184	$643,031	$316,332	$283,248

For the swap, the safety is dominant; for the option the variance is dominant. Of the two, the option risk load is smaller, and hence preferred.

TABLE 1

VALUES FOR THE OPTION TECHNIQUE

Time	1	2	3	4
Option rate	3.18%	4.49%	5.50%	6.35%
Risk load	$ 235,225	$ 316,332	$ 399,548	$ 502,444
Risk-loaded premium	$ 1,200,476	$ 1,248,042	$ 1,298,882	$ 1,370,526
Total premium	$ 1,379,857	$ 1,434,531	$ 1,492,967	$ 1,575,317
Allocated assets	$ 32,522,839	$ 23,024,033	$ 20,095,065	$ 19,446,192
Initial investment	$ 32,685,050	$ 23,228,830	$ 20,278,801	$ 19,574,132
Determining constraint	variance	variance	safety	safety
Safety value	3,087 years	1,309 years	1,000 years	1,000 years
Annualized std/target std	100%	100%	97%	93%

[8] Preferred from the point of view of the cedent, and preferred from the point of view of offering competitive advantage to the reinsurer - less charge for the same return and risk. On the other hand, the reinsurer may prefer to charge more if the market will bear it. Of course, a higher market rate can always be recast as a more profitable target investment return.

For example, in the second column of the table, time is taken as two years. Following the formulae and notation of the appendices, the investment $2\mu = 9.69\%$ and $\sigma\sqrt{2} = 11.26\%$ at two years. The target investment mean and standard deviation are 10.88% and 12.53% as calculated from the lognormal formulae. The option rate is 4.49%. The mean and standard deviation of the option-protected investment are 14.21% and 8.95%, respectively, higher and lower than the target, as previously advertised. The investment minimum value is 7.33%, the risk-free cumulative return.

The calculated risk loads and asset values are given above for both the option and the swap, and the option variance is chosen.

Please note again that any form of loss distribution could have been used, including underwriter's intuition or simulation result. All that is needed for this choice of risk load is the mean, standard deviation, and safety level. Reinsurer expenses, needed to calculate total premium from risk loaded premium, are taken as 13% of the total.

The table also lists the safety level implied by the chosen asset allocation, and the ratio of the standard deviations of the annualized yield to the target standard deviation. Whichever is not the determining constraint is, or course, more than satisfied. It is noteworthy that as the contract period becomes longer, the safety constraint becomes the more restrictive. In numerical explorations this seems generally to be true.

III.2 POOLING AND OTHER REMARKS

It is an intuitive expectation that the total risk load may be reduced by **pooling**. Pooling over contracts will be considered here; over years after the multiple payments section. The one-year contract from Table 1 has a risk load of $235,225. If there are two contracts combined into a single contract then the fixed percentage safety level used here on the combined contract is certainly less than the sum of the individual safety levels, unless the contracts are fully correlated[9]. Specifically, taking the approximation that the sum of two uncorrelated lognormals may for these purposes be represented by a lognormal, the safety level for the combined contract is $29,455,245, which is only 65.3% of the sum.

The risk load for the combined contract over one year is $331,156, which is 70.4% of the sum of the individual risk loads. This risk load results from the option variance constraint. However, one may question whether some other investment risk measure might have given a different result. The author knows of no general theorem, but experimentation has given consistent pooling.

More intuitively, both the safety levels and investment risk measures will be primarily sensitive to the tail of the loss distribution. When two contracts are imperfectly correlated, the bulk of the tail results from one or the other of the contracts going bad,

[9] Or effectively taken as such, as in the high excess example.

and not both. The effect generally is to shorten the tail relative to the mean, making measures which depend on extreme values take on less dangerous significance.

In what sense is the combination of reinsurance contract and swap/option is priced as **an equivalent investment**? A glance at the values in Table 1 shows that it is possible that if the loss is very bad, say at the 0.001% level, then the final result at the end of the time period will be negative. That is, the reinsurer will lose all the premium and allocated assets, and still have to put in more money to fulfill the contract. At the very least, this result cannot be from a lognormal distribution.

Nevertheless, it is convenient to express the mean and standard deviation of the result in terms of those of a geometric Brownian motion investment that gives the same final values. This allows a direct comparison with the original investment possibility.

To the extent that whatever investment risk measure is used is valid for general distributions, a comparison can always be made.

Should a reinsurer actually **follow through on the indicated financial technique** for each contract? Almost surely not, unless it is very conservative or this is the only contract. The latter could be the case for a specialty reinsurer set up for a single contract; for example, for a large catastrophe contract. In general, a method relating investment criteria to reinsurance contracts could be useful when specifically engineered deals are made to connect reinsureds and investors looking for new opportunities. Considering the hunger of capital for uncorrelated risks, this kind of bundling would seem natural.

This procedure takes as input the financial targets and safety criterion and produces as output the risk load and the allocated assets. It is also possible to **take the financial targets and allocated assets as input** (more the financial point of view). The two constraints then become requirements on the loss distribution. The corresponding risk loads will emerge. Knowing the desired loss characteristics and the necessary risk loads, market knowledge can be used to do selective underwriting and keep the overall distribution within acceptable risk levels at the target rate of return. This point of view is really more applicable to the book as a whole, and requires a treatment of multiple payments.

IV MULTIPLE PAYMENTS

When there are multiple loss payments possible, the same basic paradigm is used but needs a more complex formulation. In the single payment case, simultaneously enforcing the rate of return (through the mean value of the stochastic equation) and the safety constraint gave an easy solution. This will also be done here. In contrast to the single payment case, the variance constraint cannot be conveniently calculated. However, for any given level of allocated assets the variance constraint can be evaluated. If it is not satisfied, the level of allocated assets can be increased until it is, since general considerations have shown that this is always possible.

The general procedure will be: (1) Express the fundamental stochastic process on a spreadsheet. It is now more than a simple equation because of the interaction of the fund levels at different times, but it is still easily expressed. (2) Define the safety levels. (3) Use those to define what funds are needed and what options need to be bought. The swap case will not be shown in the example, but is an easier problem and follows the same procedure. (4) Find the risk load corresponding to the target return for the indicated safety constraint by putting all the stochastic variables at their mean values. (5) Simulate to see if the variance constraint is satisfied. (6) If it is not, then add "excess capital" and simulate again. (7) Repeat step (6) until both constraints are satisfied.

The procedure will be illustrated by a two-year example. The same investment parameters are used as before and the loss has mean $2M spread over two years, in a 50-50 ratio.

IV.1 LOSS SAFETY CONSTRAINT

A procedure for the safety constraint will be illustrated by reference to Table 2 below.

TABLE 2

DEVELOPMENT OF SAFETY CONSTRAINT

Time	1	2
Loss mean	$ 1,000,000	$ 1,000,000
Discounted loss mean	$ 965,251	$ 931,709
Loss std	$ 2,000,000	$ 2,000,000
Loss mu	13.0108	13.0108
Loss sigma	1.2686	1.2686
Individual safety level	$ 22,548,702	$ 22,548,702
Cumulative mean	$ 1,000,000	$ 2,036,000
Cumulative std	$ 2,000,000	$ 2,879,789
Cumulative sigma	1.2686	1.0482
Cumulative safety	$ 22,548,702	$ 29,991,527
Discounted safety	$ 21,765,156	$ 27,943,389
Initial investments	$ 21,765,156	$ 6,178,233
Cumulative option rate	3.20%	4.49%
Option cost on initial investment	$ 691,386	$ 277,474

The first is the mean of each loss, taken to happen at year-end. The next line is the mean value discounted back to time zero at the risk-free rate. The next line is the standard deviation of each loss. For ease of replicability, the partial payment distributions here are taken as lognormal with the coefficient of variation = 2, as before. The "mu" and "sigma" parameters for the lognormals are in the next two lines. The corresponding thousand-year levels are shown subsequently.

The years are also taken as uncorrelated with each other.[10] There is, however, a slight twist in this calculation: The dedicated reader will have noticed that the mean of the cumulative distribution for year two is not just the sum of the individual years one and two. The time value of money for the loss in year one must be accounted for with an appropriate rate to be comparable to a loss in year two, and to be able to add them. Since the reinsurer can think of this as borrowing from itself, the rate taken is the risk-free rate. In the swap case, this is obvious, since the securities held are risk-free. In the option case this still seems appropriate, since the lower limit which will be realized is the risk-free rate. Similarly, the standard deviation is also inflated to give the cumulative value.

In this example, for the purpose of estimating safety levels the cumulative loss distributions, which are the sum of lognormal distributions, are assumed themselves lognormal and the parameters calculated. Simulation runs show that the resulting safety levels are close enough to use.

The cumulative safety levels, however arrived at, are discounted back to zero at the risk-free rate. Thinking in terms of the swap, one could just take the largest[11] of these numbers as the initial fund required. This will fulfill the guarantee to have the safety level liquid at all times. It will also mean that much of the time there will be (expensive) excess liquidity available.

For the option case it will be useful to think of different parts of the initial investment as relating to different time periods. Consider the year two cumulative safety level. Part of it will come from the year one level, increased by investment income at the risk-free rate. The next row, "initial investments", shows the amounts to be invested at time zero in order to have their cumulative value be the safety levels at different times. In the example here the second entry is just the difference between the discounted safety levels.

Options are considered to be purchased separately at time zero on each part of the total at, of course, different costs. The next row "cumulative option rate" shows the rates[12] for options out to the various times, and the last row is the dollar costs of these options.

---

[10] This is only a convenience. The mean and standard deviations of these cumulative loss distributions are easily calculated with correlation.

[11] In the current example, the largest discounted cumulative safety level is the last. However, in the next table and example is given where it is the first.

[12] These are the same rates as in Table 1.

It is useful to look also at another example, which is only changed by having the losses come in at 95% and 5% in the first and second year respectively. This is shown in Table 2A below:

TABLE 2A

DEVELOPMENT OF SAFETY CONSTRAINT

Time	1	2
Loss mean	$ 1,900,000	$ 100,000
Discounted loss mean	$ 1,833,977	$ 93,171
Loss std	$ 3,800,000	$ 200,000
Loss mu	13.6526	10.7082
Loss sigma	1.2686	1.2686
Individual safety level	$ 42,842,533	$ 2,254,870
Cumulative mean	$ 1,900,000	$ 2,068,400
Cumulative std	$ 3,800,000	$ 3,941,877
Cumulative sigma	1.2686	1.2381
Cumulative safety	$ 42,842,533	$ 44,098,350
Discounted safety	$ 41,353,796	$ 41,086,848
Initial investments	$ 41,353,796	$ 0
Cumulative option rate	3.20%	4.49%
Option cost on initial investments	$ 1,313,633	$ 0

IV.2 STOCHASTIC SPREADSHEET AT AVERAGE VALUES

With the preceding as preparation, Table 3 can be constructed, which describes the spreadsheet with all stochastic variables at average values. The two-period hedged investment return is 14.21%. The risk load is obtained by asking[13] that it be an amount such that when all the stochastic processes are at their average values the desired target results.

[13] This can be done by trial and error, but is more easily done by "Goal Seek" or its equivalent in the spreadsheet.

TABLE 3

STOCHASTIC PROCESSES AT THEIR AVERAGE VALUES

time	0	1	2
assets	**$27,172,116**	$28,612,238	$30,128,686
excess investment	**$0**		
risk load	**$329,782**		
premium	**$2,226,742**		
option cost	**$984,364**		
invested	**$28,414,494**		
Fund 01	**$22,236,261**	$23,978,898	
Fund 02	**$6,178,233**	#N/A	$7,056,055
loss 1		$1,000,000	
funds available		$22,978,898	
desired Fund 12		**$15,364,507**	
actual Fund 12		$15,364,507	$16,568,610
option rate 1 to 2		**3.177%**	
Fund12 option cost		$488,065	
funds released		$7,126,326	$7,504,021
loss 2			$1,000,000
result			$30,128,686

The assets allocated are given at the top. The method to get them is described below. The target investment value given the assets at time 0 is $30,128,686. The first row shows what would have happened on average if the assets had simply been invested.

The "excess investment" is the amount above that required for the safety constraint. At the moment, it is zero.

The "premium" is the sum of the discounted mean losses plus the risk load. The option cost is the cost of options on the investment. It is the sum of the costs shown in Table 2, plus a piece to be described later in this section. "Invested" is assets plus premium less the option cost. It is also the sum of "Fund01" and "Fund02". The Fund01 is the investment at time 0 to be used at time 1; similarly for Fund02.

In order to discuss Fund01, it is necessary to describe the process envisioned and the options which will be bought at different times. At time zero, the safety levels are evaluated and their option costs determined as in Table 2. There are two different options: one assures the initial investment needed for the cumulative safety level at time 1 will reach it at time 1. The other assures that the difference of the discounted cumulative safety levels will reach its desired value at time 2. There is nothing yet to assure that the funds invested to reach the cumulative safety level at time one will actually grow at the risk-free rate from time 1 to time 2.

Let "desired Fund12" be the amount at time 1 which when hedged will grow from time 1 to time 2 so that the sum of it and the mature Fund02 will be the cumulative safety level at time 2 evaluated at time 1, as seen from time zero. Specifically for the example, at time 1 loss 1 has already come in so only loss 2 is relevant. The safety level desired is the individual safety level of $22,548,702. The $6,178,233 invested will mature to $6,631,072, so the difference is $15,917,629. Discounted back one period, the desired Fund12 is $15,364,507. The projected option cost of desired Fund12 is $488,065, which is paid at time 1. The option cost discounted to time zero is $471,105.

Thus, Fund01 contains both the initial investment for the safety level at time 1 of $21,765,156 and the Fund12 option cost of $471,105. The cost of the one year option bought to cover Fund01 is then $691,386 from Table 2 plus the option cost on $471,105. The latter is the extra piece of the option cost referred to earlier.

At this point, Fund02 only contains the entry from Table 2 for the difference in the discounted cumulative safety levels. This is everything at time zero.

At time 1, Fund01 has grown to $23,978,898 and loss 1 has come in at $1,000,000. After paying the loss, the "funds available" of $22,978,898 exceed the desired Fund12 of $15,364,507 so the "actual Fund12" can be equal to the desired. The "Fund12 option cost", paid at this time, to take it to time 2 is the aforementioned $488,065. The funds available less actual Fund12 less its option cost is $7,126,326, which is the "funds released" to the unhedged target investment.

At time 2, the mature Fund02 is available. It will on average[14] have grown faster than the risk-free rate, as will the actual Fund12, so that their sum here will exceed the safety level of $22,548,702. Summing to the bottom (subtracting loss 2) the final result of the contracts is seen. As mentioned earlier, at the average values used here the risk load is chosen so that this final result is the same as if the assets had simply been invested, shown in the top line.

[14] It is to be noted that the two year average hedged investment will be at a larger rate than the compounded one year average, because of the possibility of very low returns one year being offset by high returns the next.

IV.3 STOCHASTIC SPREADSHEET AND VARIANCE

When the stochastic variables are not at their average values, the general flow is the same. Table 4 below shows a fairly atypical sample simulation, in that only 5.8% of the time will the available funds be less than the desired Fund12.

TABLE 4

SAMPLE SIMULATION

time	0	1	2
assets	**$27,172,116**	$32,968,038	$35,108,232
excess investment	**$0**		
risk load	**$329,782**		
premium	**$2,226,742**		
option cost	**$984,364**		
invested	**$28,414,494**		
Fund 01	**$22,236,261**	$26,979,345	
Fund 02	**$6,178,233**	#N/A	$7,982,699
loss 1		$15,149,162	
funds available		$11,830,183	
desired Fund 12		**$15,364,507**	
actual Fund 12		$11,465,959	$12,210,298
option rate 1 to 2		**3.177%**	
Fund12 option cost		$364,225	
funds released		$0	$0
loss 2			$1,118,584
result			$19,074,413

The values in the table that do not change over different simulations are shown in **bold**, such as the assets at time 0. In this particular simulation, the investments did very well. The first row shows what would have happened if the assets had simply been invested. However, the good investment returns were not able to offset the large loss at time 1 completely, so that the final result is well under the target value of $30,128,686.

The actual Fund12 needs more discussion. The simplest way to do the actual Fund12 would be to make it equal to the desired Fund12. In this case, that would mean re-allocating investments from elsewhere. However, the whole spirit here has been to allocate the investments up front, and not put more in until they were exhausted. The usefulness of a safety level is that is makes explicit, at least indirectly, the minimum funds to be allocated. Unless the safety level is 100%, there is always the possibility (which will occur in some simulations) that more will be required, but the intent is to run with what was allocated as long as possible.

Hence, the rule followed in this spreadsheet is that the actual Fund12 is the desired Fund12 if there are enough funds available at time 1, or whatever positive fund can be generated from the funds available (which is the case here). In most simulations, there will be more than enough funds available to generate the desired Fund12, and funds will be released back to the reinsurer to be invested in the target investment. In some simulations, there will be positive funds available, and they are used to create Fund12 and pay for the option; but no funds are released.

In a few simulations (about 0.6% in the example) with rather large losses, there will be negative funds available. In this situation Fund12 will be zero and the funds released will be negative. The interpretation is that the reinsurer will have to supply funds from the target investment. It is assumed that the Fund02 will not be available until time 2; but in any case it is earning on average more than the target anyway and it would not be profitable to cash it in.

With the spreadsheet defined, it is now possible to run simulations and evaluate the risk measure—here the standard deviation. With the example parameters the variance of the final result is 13.28%. This corresponds for a lognormal investment to a standard deviation of 8.91%[15].

If the standard deviation is smaller than the target value, then the safety constraint is the more restrictive. If not, then adding excess investment over the full time horizon will reduce the variance while still satisfying the safety constraint. Here, the target is 8.4%, so some "excess investment" must be added to reduce the variance. A first approximation can be obtained by noting that the standard deviation must be reduced about 6% which suggests increasing the investments by 6%. Accordingly, the excess investment was set to $1,800,000. The risk load that corresponds is a slight increase to $342,513. In the fund development, this excess investment lives in Fund02, and is option protected. The revised spreadsheet gives an investment-equivalent standard deviation of 8.31%. Since this is below the target, it is acceptable[16].

IV.4 COMMENTS ON THE SPREADSHEET

There are other possible ways of setting up the spreadsheet. **A general rule that should be satisfied is if the payment stream is essentially zero except at one time, the results for the risk load and the allocated assets should reduce to the single-payment case.**

A corollary is that funds must be able to be released: consider the case of a ten year contract with 99.9% of the payments in the first year. If the cumulative safety level as

[15] On 200,000 simulations. The values for 10,000 and 40,000 simulations were 8.16% and 9.00%. The size of this variation indicated the need for many more simulations.

[16] In order to go further, as the difference from the target gets smaller a much larger number of simulations needs to be done. The simulation uncertainty must be smaller than the difference between the result and the target. Preferably much smaller.

seen at time 0 were maintained for the full ten years, then when the first year loss is not at an extreme value the safety level maintained would be far too high—and therefore too expensive to maintain. The safety level must be revisited after each loss, and funds released when appropriate. On the other hand, if the first year loss *is* near an extreme value to take the subsequent safety levels at the values they would have had for a small first-year loss is to allow for a much more stringent safety condition than was originally intended.

It is for these reasons that the procedure was defined as above and the actual Fund12 is not always the desired Fund12 as defined. A more sophisticated version for the case where the safety level is done on straight probability levels for loss would be to use conditional probabilities and take into account how much probability of the 99.9% level the first loss had used up, followed by the second, and so on. However, the current version is relatively simple and probably accurate enough, especially given the parameter uncertainty inherent in the various aspects of the problem.

There is a difficulty with the current approach to the actual Fund12. It is that when we take average value of the stochastic inputs to the spreadsheet, it does not give average values to the spreadsheet and the resulting risk load is slightly low. The reason is that the average value of actual Fund12 is slightly below the desired Fund12, and not at it which is the result seen in Table 3. This difficulty can be overcome either by going to the simple version of the actual Fund12 treatment or by using the simulation results on the rate to readjust the risk load.

The above procedure for the two-period case may be extended to multiple periods, each with its own loss distribution. The desired funds are the results of the original safety criterion as seen at each period in time. Thus, for a four year problem there will be successively Funds01,02,03,04; desired Funds12,13,14; actual Funds12,13,14; desired Funds23,24; actual Funds23,24; desired Fund34; and actual Fund34. The discounted option costs for the desired FundNM is in Fund0N and any excess investment is in Fund04.

V GENERAL REMARKS

Generalizations: For convenience the losses are taken to happen at the end of each year, although there is no essential difficulty in generalizing to arbitrary times. Also, since simulations are being run any measures of risk and return which can be defined on individual results can be used.

A few words about **IRR and future value**: In the single payment case the IRR was used because it is unequivocally defined, and provides a natural way of talking about returns. It was not actually necessary to look at the IRR and only the end result need have been considered. In the multiple payment case the IRR may not even be definable as a real number. This is particularly obvious when the final value is negative because of large losses, but can also happen otherwise. In order to consider the end value (future value of the cash flows) it is necessary to set up some description of the investment policy on the released funds. The target investment is the obvious choice.

An inessential simplification used here is to ignore the fact that the **spot rates** for risk-free investment depend upon the length of time considered, usually rising with time. For example, incremental losses could be discounted back to time zero using the different spot rates. Here only one single risk-free rate is assumed to apply, for all times of the contract. However, if a reinsurer so desires, then the calculations can be straightforwardly reformulated to include the current spot rates and the view of what the future values of the spot rates are likely to be over the contract period.

It is intuitive that there should be a reduction from **pooling over years**, even allowing for the increased cost of liquidity of the later contract. The example in Tables 3 and 4 is two uncorrelated contracts, and the risk load of $342,513 is less than the twice the single contract value of $235,225 and comparable to the $331,156 for a two simultaneous contracts. Again, the author knows of no general theorem, but experimentation seems to indicate that pooling over time is usually present for uncorrelated contracts.

In real-world scenarios, however, the individual years of multi-year contracts may well have some correlation simply because they are from the same firm or exposures. In the simulation environment, there is no difficulty evaluating the overall contract if one has some idea of the correlation.

The pricing here is **extreme pricing** in that each contract is priced as a stand-alone entity, whereas in reality each contract is supported by the whole surplus of the reinsurer. A more accurate treatment of the actual risk load needed to satisfy investment criteria would be to consider the whole book with and without the proposed contract. Perhaps a satisfactory compromise would be to scale the extreme risk load contemplated here by the ratio of the overall portfolio risk charge to the sum of the extreme risk loads.

Many thanks are due to Gary Venter, the reviewer, and Mike Steel for valuable input and discussions.

APPENDICES

Appendix 1

The form of the Black-Scholes formula for the price of a European call option on a security is[17]

$$\text{call price} = \Phi(\Delta_1)P_0 - \Phi(\Delta_2)PV(E)$$

where $PV(E)$ = present value of the exercise price discounted at the risk-free rate,

P_0 = price of the security at time zero,

$$\Delta_1 = \frac{\ln\left(\dfrac{P_0}{PV(E)}\right)}{\sigma\sqrt{t}} + \frac{\sigma\sqrt{t}}{2}$$

$$\Delta_2 = \Delta_1 - \sigma\sqrt{t}$$

where σ is a parameter of the distribution of the underlying security and is $\Phi(x)$ the cumulative distribution function for the normal distribution, that is

$$\Phi(x) = \int_{-\infty}^{x} \frac{e^{-z^2/2}}{\sqrt{2\pi}} dz.$$

This function is available in at least one standard spreadsheet program.

The option is the right to buy the underlying security at the exercise price at the time t. The logarithm of the value of the security is assumed to follow a normal distribution with parameters μt and $\sigma\sqrt{t}$ for the mean and standard deviation, respectively[18]. Given the expected annual yield rate y and its standard deviation σ_y, then

$$\sigma^2 = \ln\left\{1 + \left(\frac{\sigma_y}{1+y}\right)^2\right\}$$

---

[17]Brealey and Myers, op. cit., page 502

[18]This is known as a geometric Wiener process or geometric Brownian motion process. See the development of Black-Scholes in "Stochastic Methods is Economics and Finance" by Malliaris and Brock (North-Holland, 1982) on pages 220-223, and the discussion of the Brownian motion on pages 36-38, especially equation (7.13) and the development leading to it.

and

$$\mu = \ln(1+y) - \frac{\sigma^2}{2}$$

The price for a put option, which is actually what is of interest here, is given by put-call parity as

$$\text{put price} = \text{call price} + PV(E) - P_0$$

In the case of interest here $PV(E) = P_0$ since we want the exercise price to be the growth at the risk-free rate. Hence the put price is equal to the call price, and for either option the

$$\text{option cost} = P_0 \Phi\left(\frac{\sigma\sqrt{t}}{2}\right) - P_0 \Phi\left(-\frac{\sigma\sqrt{t}}{2}\right)$$

so the

$$\text{option rate} = \Phi\left(\frac{\sigma\sqrt{t}}{2}\right) - \Phi\left(-\frac{\sigma\sqrt{t}}{2}\right)$$

Or,

$$\text{option rate} = \sqrt{\frac{2}{\pi}} \int_0^{\sigma\sqrt{t}/2} e^{-z^2/2} dz .$$

The exponential may be expanded to first order in a Taylor series to get the approximation quoted, which is actually rather good for the order of magnitude of numbers used here.

Appendix 2

As stated in appendix 1, the probability density function for the investment value (which is 1+return) is lognormal with parameters μt and $\sigma\sqrt{t}$. That is,

$$f(x) = \frac{1}{\sigma x \sqrt{2\pi t}} \exp\left\{\frac{-\left(\ln(x) - \mu t\right)^2}{\sigma^2 t}\right\}.$$

The investment hedged with the option to time t has the characteristics (f is the risk-free rate)

$$\begin{aligned} \text{investment} &= x && \text{for} \quad x \geq (1+f)^t \\ &= (1+f)^t && \text{for} \quad x < (1+f)^t. \end{aligned}$$

What is needed are the moments of the investment; in particular its mean and standard deviation.

Define

$$\begin{aligned} F_n &= \int_0^{(1+f)^t} x^n f(x)dx \\ &= \Phi\left(\zeta - n\sigma\sqrt{t}\right)\exp\left\{n\mu t + n^2\sigma^2 t/2\right\} \end{aligned}$$

where

$$\zeta = \sqrt{t}\left\{\frac{\ln(1+f) - \mu}{\sigma}\right\}.$$

In general,

$$\begin{aligned} \text{moment}(n) &= \int_0^{\infty} \text{investment}^n f(x)dx \\ &= (1+f)^{nt} \int_0^{(1+f)^t} f(x)dx + \int_{(1+f)^t}^{\infty} x^n f(x)dx \end{aligned}$$

Using the results for F_n above, the moment of order n of the investment is

$$\begin{aligned} \text{moment}(n) &= (1+f)^{nt} F_0 + \exp\left(n\mu t + n^2\sigma^2 t/2\right) - F_n \\ &= (1+f)^{nt} \Phi(\zeta) + \exp\left(n\mu t + n^2\sigma^2 t/2\right)\left[1 - \Phi\left(\zeta - n\sigma\sqrt{t}\right)\right] \end{aligned}$$

The mean value is just moment(1) and the variance of the investment is {moment(2) - moment(1)^2}.

APPENDIX 3

Derivation of Eq. (5): Substitute for μ_L and F in Eq. (4):

Eq. (1) may be solved for μ_L as

(A.1) $$\mu_L = (1+r_f)(P-R)$$

Substitute F from Eq. (2) and L from Eq. (A.1) into Eq. (4):

(4) $$\begin{aligned}(1+y)A &= (1+r_f)(P+A)-(1+r_f)(P-R)\\ &= (1+r_f)A+(1+r_f)R\end{aligned}$$

Solving for R gives Eq. (5).

Derivation of Eq. (21):

Eq. (17) can be written

$$(1+r)F = P + A = A + \frac{\mu_L}{(1+r_f)} + R$$

from Eq. (1). Rearranging to solve for R, and subsequently using Eq. (6) for F and Eq. (20) for A,

$$\begin{aligned}R &= (1+r)F - A - \frac{\mu_L}{(1+r_f)}\\ &= (1+r)\frac{S}{1+r_f} - \frac{1}{1+y}\left(\frac{1+i}{1+r_f}S - \mu_L\right) - \frac{\mu_L}{1+r_f}\\ &= \frac{S}{1+r_f}\left[(1+r) - \frac{1+i}{1+y}\right] + \mu_L\left[\frac{1}{1+y} - \frac{1}{1+r_f}\right]\\ &= \frac{1}{(1+r_f)(1+y)}\left[S\left\{(1+y)(1+r_f)-(1+i)\right\} - \mu_L\left\{y-r_f\right\}\right]\end{aligned}$$

Derivation of Eqs. (23)-(26):

Eq. (19) can be written

$$F = \frac{(1+y)A + \mu_L}{1+i}$$

Substituting for F in Eq. (22) gives

$$A^2\sigma_y^2 = \left[(1+y)^2 A^2 + 2A\mu_L(1+y) + \mu_L^2\right]\frac{\sigma_i^2}{(1+i)^2} + \sigma_L^2$$

Multiplying through by the denominator and collecting terms,

$$0 = A^2\left[(1+y)^2\sigma_i^2 - \sigma_y^2(1+i)^2\right] + 2A\mu_L(1+y)\sigma_i^2 + \mu_L^2\sigma_i^2 + \sigma_L^2(1+i)^2$$

This is Eqs. (23)-(26). If there is a correlation ρ_{iL} between investment and loss, then this equation becomes

$$0 = A^2\left[(1+y)^2\sigma_i^2 - \sigma_y^2(1+i)^2\right] + 2A(1+y)\sigma_i\left[\mu_L\sigma_i + \sigma_{iL}(1+i)\right]$$
$$+ \mu_L^2\sigma_i^2 + \sigma_L^2(1+i)^2 + 2\mu_L\sigma_i\sigma_L(1+i)\rho_{iL}$$

Derivation of Eq. (28):

By substituting for F from Eq. (17) into Eq. (19)

$$(1+y)A = (1+i)\frac{P+A}{1+r} - \mu_L$$

Multiplying through by the denominator and using Eq. (1) for P,

$$A(1+y)(1+r) = (1+i)\left(R + \frac{\mu_L}{1+r_f} + A\right) - \mu_L(1+r)$$

Rearranging terms,

$$(1+r) = A\left[(1+y(1+r) - (1+i)\right] + \mu_L\left[(1+r) - \frac{1+i}{1+r_f}\right]$$

Eq. (28) for R results immediately.

CHAPTER SEVEN
THEORETICAL PREMIUMS FOR PROPERTY AND CASUALTY INSURANCE COVERAGE - A RISK-SENSITIVE, TOTAL RETURN APPROACH

By Ira Robbin

OVERVIEW

The purpose of this paper is to present a conceptual paradigm for deriving the premium for a property or casualty insurance policy. The essential idea is that the premium should be sufficient to generate an adequate total return to the investors who supplied necessary capital to the insurance company that issued the policy.

In presenting this approach and some of its implications, the focus will be on the theory and concepts. No real world applications will be demonstrated and no suggestion will be made on how to price any particular coverage. Nor will there be any attempt to debate the merits of this approach versus any other or argue whether it is appropriate for use in any rate hearing or other forum.

THE NEED FOR CAPITAL

An insurance company needs a sufficient supply of capital in order to provide meaningful insurance protection. Without such capital behind it, the company issuing an insurance policy is making a promise of coverage it may be unable to fulfill. If losses are above expectation and if the company has inadequate funds to cover such adverse deviation, it may then have to default on its obligation to pay losses.

Insurance regulators in the United States have recognized the importance of adequate capitalization in ensuring that such defaults occur as infrequently as possible. They have established capital benchmarks and taken action against companies capitalized below minimum standards. In recent years, simple rules of thumb such as the "3-to-1" premium-to-surplus ratio have been replaced by the more sophisticated "Risk-Based Capital" formula as regulators push for more accurate and timely approaches to solvency regulations. Insurance company rating agencies have also focused on adequacy of capitalization as a key factor in determining company ratings.

In addition to establishing benchmarks, regulators have also mandated that companies use a conservative set of accounting rules, Statutory Accounting Principles (SAP), in evaluating their actual capital. The intent of SAP accounting is to make sure that an insurance company has enough cash and easily liquidated assets on hand to pay off all obligations even if the company were shut down the next day. Under the "balance sheet, liquidation" perspective of statutory Accounting, some assets may be understated and some liabilities may be overstated relative to their values under the "income statement, going-concern" perspective of Generally Accepted Accounting Principles (GAAP) or the true economic approaches used by some financial analysts in evaluating acquisitions and mergers.

An important consequence of the conservative accounting rules is that they keep money in the insurance company that might otherwise be given to investors. In particular, when premiums are paid to an insurance company, the investors of the company do not get their hands on the cash. Rather, most of the funds stay with the company as assets to offset liabilities posted for premiums, claims, and expenses. Not only do they not get the cash, but also investors may find some of their invested capital gets absorbed in keeping the company adequately capitalized under a conservative accounting regimen. For example, under SAP, a significant portion of the expense is declared up-front when a policy is written even though associated premiums will be earned evenly over the policy term. This results in a double-counting of expenses which dissipates as the premium is earned. In GAAP, there is an asset account, the Deferred Acquisition Costs (DAC) balance, which is posted to offset this "equity in the unearned premium reserve". The key point here is that some investor capital does not show up in the SAP valuation of the company's surplus. Because accounting rules tie up money that could go to insurance company investors, they impact the return investors obtain on their investment in the company.

THE INVESTORS' PERSPECTIVE

Consider a hypothetical scenario in which investors are looking at the merits of an investment in a fictitious insurance company formed for the sole purpose of writing a single property or casualty insurance policy. Suppose company management intends to charge a specified premium rate and an actuary has supplied estimates of expected losses and expenses to be paid out. Assume the timing of all payments is forecast as accurately as current methods permit. Suppose interest rates and income taxes are known. Would that be enough for the potential investors to make a decision? Of course not! Because knowing the company's cash flows to and from policyholders, tax collection agencies, agents, employees, and so forth is all very interesting to investors, but not nearly as interesting as the projected flow of funds between the company and the investors themselves. The investors want to know about the moneys they will put in and get out. Also, the investors want to know how risky the deal is.

EQUITY FLOWS

To formalize this, assume investors incorporate a fictitious company set up to write a single insurance policy. Let the term *equity flow* denote movements of cash between a company and its investors. A negative equity flow, denoting the transfer of money into the company by the investors, could take the form of a purchase of company stock by the investors. A positive equity flow might consist of dividends on stock or a repurchase of shares. An initial negative equity flow would occur at policy inception as investors put up money so that the company has enough capital to write the policy. If the company's books were tabulated just after the policy was written, they would probably show, under the conservative rules of statutory accounting, that the company has less surplus than the capital put in by the investors. At the end of each accounting period, income would be declared and a provisional balance sheet would be computed. Ignoring changes to surplus that do not flow through the income statement (such as unrealized capital gains), the provisional surplus would differ from the surplus at the end of the prior accounting period by the declared income. However, if company management saw that it would have more than sufficient surplus so as to probably stay solvent over the next accounting period, it might decide to pay some money to investors. This would generate a positive equity flow. If the provisional balance sheet looked weak, management might try to get investors to put in more money so that there would be a negative equity flow. After the equity flow, the balance sheet would show a period-to-period change in surplus equal to the sum of income less the equity flow. Rewriting the equation we see that equity flow is equal to income less the change in surplus. Thus, if we had the prospective books for the hypothetical company showing its income and its surplus for each accounting period, we could calculate the prospective flows of money to and from its investors.

IRR ON EQUITY FLOWS

Investors could measure profitability of any projected outcome of a venture by computing the Internal Rate of Return (IRR) on the equity flows. Assuming annual time periods, the IRR is that rate (if it exists and is unique) at which the present value of the equity flows (*EQF*) is zero:

$$IRR = y \text{ if and only if } \sum \mathrm{EQF_j}(1+y)^{-j} = 0$$

The *IRR* on equity flows is a measure of return directly comparable with the interest rate on a bond. For example, if the equity flows are -110, +11, +121, the *IRR* is 10% since $0 = -100 + 11\cdot(1.1)^{-1} + 121\cdot(1.1)^{-2}$.

TARGET RETURN

Applying a risk-return paradigm in an insurance context, one could say that a theoretically justified premium should lead to an expected IRR equal to an appropriate risk-sensitive target return. This target return should at least equal the pre-tax risk-free yield otherwise available to investors. However, as will be discussed below, when investors put money in an insurance company, the impact of income taxes and statutory accounting tends to push their return below this floor. Thus, part of the premium is needed merely to raise the expected return to an acceptable non-risk adjusted level.

How much to boost the target return for risk is a question subject to debate. For the sake of argument, suppose the insurance company only invests in risk-free bonds, that it matches the duration of its investment against its liabilities so as to partly immunize itself from interest rate fluctuation, and further suppose that losses for the policy are entirely uncorrelated with returns on the stock market. Under these assumptions, it follows that, approximately, the IRR to investors will have a zero covariance with the stock market return. If that were true, then one could argue under a strict CAPM approach that the target return ought to be equal to the risk-free return and no higher!

OFFSET FOR INCOME TAXES ON INVESTMENT INCOME

Suppose the company writes no insurance policies, but merely takes the funds invested in it and then reinvests them at the risk-free rate. Because the company must pay income taxes before distributing proceeds to its investors, it will be able to provide investors with a return only equal to the after-tax risk-free yield. Thus, even without consideration of risk, the profit load ought to contain an offset making up for income taxes on the investment income on assets supplied by the equity investors. In effect, the taxes on this investment income have to be passed through to policyholders.

OFFSET FOR CONSERVATISM IN STATUTORY ACCOUNTING

Due the conservative nature of statutory accounting, the investors do not get potential profits as quickly as they otherwise might. Further, they have more invested in the venture than the statutory surplus would indicate. This has implications on their return from the venture. Consider, from a pure cash flow perspective, the surplus of the company might be valued as the difference between the current market value of its assets less the present value of expected subsequent underwriting outflows. However, statutory surplus is the difference between statutory assets and statutory liabilities, and statutory liabilities are usually much greater than the present value of subsequent underwriting outflows. Loss and loss expense reserves are usually supposed to be held at full value. Also, the posting of unearned premium reserves leads in effect to the double-counting of expenses. This is the source of the "equity in the unearned premium reserve" or the balance for Deferred Acquisition Costs recognized in GAAP.

While funds that could, from a strict cash flow perspective, be paid out as profits languish in insurance company vaults offsetting statutory liabilities, they earn investment income. However, here again, income taxes reduce the return on those funds. Thus, to get a sufficiently attractive total return, the premium must implicitly include a charge for the substandard yield on the delayed remission of profits. **The extra protection afforded to policyholders by the discipline of statutory accounting does not come cost-free. One main omission in several pure cash-flow approaches to insurance pricing lies in the failure to reflect the impact of accounting rules on the flow of cash to investors.**

RISK AND SURPLUS

To investors, risk pertains to the possibility they will not get the return they expected on their investment. To policyholders, on the other hand, risk relates to the possibility the insurance company will run out of money and default on payments of covered loss. Running the company with more surplus does not change the underlying risk of adverse loss experience, but it does decrease the risk to policyholders.

In order to reflect the level of capitalization, consider a "Target Surplus" model in which surplus is capped by pre-set targets that evolve over the life of the policy according to pre-set rules. Investors will put up enough initially so that carried surplus is equal to the target when the policy is written. Subsequently, carried surplus could fall below target if results are less rosy than initially hoped. In that event, future profits will be used to build the carried surplus back up to the target. If results are very poor, the company could run through its surplus and go bankrupt. The odds of this happening are inversely related to the level of target surplus.

A critical point is that the targets on surplus function to cap the surplus and thus ensure that accumulated profits and excess surplus will be returned to investors. If surplus amasses to momentarily exceed the target amount, the company's management will immediately send the extra surplus back to the investors in the form of capital distributions or dividends. Further assume the cap on surplus eventually declines to zero so that no funds that could go to investors are kept from them indefinitely.

THE IRR DISTRIBUTION

Based on a set of surplus targets, loss distribution and payout assumptions, reserving accuracy assumptions, investment and tax assumptions, and so forth, one could in principle derive a distribution of IRR's. This distribution of returns should provide investors with sufficient information to decide if the venture is sufficiently lucrative relative to the risk involved. To simplify matters, assume that the standard deviation of the IRR provides an adequate measure of risk.

PREMIUM AND TARGET SURPLUS IMPACT IRR DISTRIBUTION AND RISK TO POLICYHOLDERS

As a hypothetical example of how changes in premium and target surplus impact the odds of default on obligations to policyholders and on the expected IRR and standard deviation of IRR to investors, consider the following chart of hypothetical results:

TABLE 1

Premium	Target Surplus	Default Odds	Expected IRR	IRR Std Dev
$100	Very High	0.01%	6.00%	4.00%
$100	High	0.10%	7.00%	6.00%
$100	Medium	0.51%	9.00%	9.00%
$100	Low	1.01%	15.00%	15.00%
$105	Very High	0.01%	7.50%	4.00%
$105	High	0.10%	10.50%	6.00%
$105	Medium	0.50%	15.50%	9.00%
$105	Low	1.00%	24.50%	15.00%

Note the amount of premium has a tiny impact on the default odds. Also, observe the amount of premium has no impact on the standard deviation of IRR. The reasoning here is that variations about the average IRR are driven by variations in loss and investment results relative to the surplus and not by the premium level.

It is straightforward that more surplus reduces the risk of default on obligations to policyholders. Target surplus also impacts the expected return. Due to the "leverage" of capital, an increase in surplus moves returns towards the after-tax yield on investments made by the company. In the example above, all returns are apparently above this after-tax yield and so increases in the target surplus lower the return. Increases in target surplus also act to reduce the standard deviation of return. This happens whether or not returns are above or below the after-tax yield, as long as one assumes investment risk is less volatile than the risk of adverse loss experience.

If the risk-free pre-tax yield was 7.2%, the $100 premium would entice no investors if they had to fund the "high" or "very high" surplus targets. However, they could perhaps be enticed by the "medium" or "low" target surplus ventures. Raising the premium to $105 might get some to put up funds to cover the "high" or "very high" surplus targets.

Abstracting from this, it follows that premiums consistent with this model will vary with the level of surplus: the higher the surplus target, the higher the premium. What the policyholder gets for the higher premium is a greater assurance that all claims will be paid.

CONCLUSION

Under the theory expounded here, the premium for an insurance policy is set so as to provide investors with a total return commensurate with the risk they undertake supplying necessary funds to the insurance company. The more funds they supply, the less will be the risk to policyholders that the company will default on its obligations. Since different companies offering identical coverage operate with different levels of default risk, this theory gives no one correct price for an insurance policy. Rather, it posits a curve of prices that correspond to differing odds of default. These, in turn, are inversely related to the target level of surplus maintained by the company. What price the consumer will pay depends on how much extra the consumer wants to pay in premium now to avoid a potential default later. Since this paper has not attempted to describe consumer willingness to pay an extra price to mitigate odds of default, it is at best incomplete. Nonetheless, it is hoped this presentation of the "supply side" of insurance pricing will provide useful insights and prove a solid foundation for further analysis.

CHAPTER EIGHT
INSURANCE PROFITABILITY

By Charles L. McClenahan, FCAS, ASA, MAAA

INTRODUCTION

Measurement of profitability is to some extent, like beauty, in the eye of the beholder. The connotation of the word *profitability* is highly dependent upon who is assessing profitability and to what purpose. To investors and insurers, *profitability* has a golden ring to it. To policyholders of a stock insurer it sounds like *markup*, while to those insured by a mutual company it is neutral. Insurance regulators either encourage profitability, when concerned with solvency, or seek to curtail it, when regulating rates. The IRS seeks to inflate it and consumer groups seek to minimize it.

In most businesses there is a clear distinction between historical profitability, which within a given set of accounting rules and conventions is relatively well established, and prospective profitability. In the property-casualty insurance business, however, there is no such clear-cut demarcation. At the end of a year only about 40% of the incurred losses for that year will have been paid by the typical property-casualty insurer. It is several years before an insurer knows with relative certainty how much money it made or lost in a given period. When *history* depends upon the *future*, things have a tendency to become confusing.

The extent to which reported profits depend upon estimated liabilities for unpaid losses provides property-casualty insurers with some opportunity to manage reported results by strengthening or weakening loss reserves. Because deficient reserves must ultimately be strengthened and redundancies must ultimately be recognized, the interplay between current reserving decisions and the amortization of past reserving decisions adds an additional level of complexity to the problem of measuring property-casualty insurance profitability.

In this paper I will attempt to avoid staking out any position regarding the qualitative assessment of profitability. Hopefully both pro-profit readers and anti-profit readers will find my positions overwhelmingly convincing. Nor will I address the convolutions of potential reserve strengthening and weakening and the associated amortization of redundancies and deficiencies. For the sake of understanding, I will simply pretend that profitability is subject to consistent and accurate determination under a given set of accounting rules and conventions.

PROFIT V. RATE-OF-RETURN

It is important at the outset to distinguish between *profit* - the excess of revenues over expenditures - and *rate-of-return* - the ratio of profit to equity, assets, sales or some other base. Profit, no matter how uncertain, is a monetary value representing the reward to owners for putting their assets at risk and has an absolute meaning in the context of currency values. Rate-of-return is a measure of efficiency which has meaning only relative to alternative real or assumed rates-of-return.

Profit is important to investors and management as sources of dividends and growth. To insureds and regulators profits provide additional security against insolvency. Rate-of-return is important to a prospective investor as a means to compare alternative investments and to an economist as an assessment of economic efficacy. These are valid and useful functions and I do not wish to minimize their importance. But the arena in which property-casualty insurance company profitability measurement is most discussed is that of rate regulation, and this paper is written in the context of what I consider appropriate in a ratemaking or rate regulatory environment.

Since rate-of-return, however expressed, begins with profit in the numerator, it seems appropriate to begin with a discussion of the measurement of property and casualty insurance company profit.

PROFIT - RATEMAKING BASIS

While it has long been realized that the investment of policyholder-provided funds is a source of income to a property and casualty insurance company, it was not until the 1970s that such income actually constituted an important part of insurance company profit. Even today it is common to hear references to *underwriting profit*, while the investment counterpart is generally termed investment *income*, not investment *profit*. In Lewis E. David's' *Dictionary of Insurance* (Littlefield, Adams & Co., 1962) there is a definition for *Underwriting Profit* but not for *Profit*, *Investment Income*, or *Interest Income*. The International Risk Management Institute's *Glossary of Insurance and Risk Management Terms* (RCI Communications, Inc., 1980) includes both *Underwriting Profit* and *Investment Income* but continues the distinction between profit and income.

Common usage notwithstanding, there are few who would contend today that investment activities should be separate from underwriting activities in the measurement of insurance company profit. And were it not for rate regulation, statutory and GAAP accounting procedures would probably suffice for the vast majority of profit calculations. Rate regulation, however, has forced property and casualty insurers to make a somewhat artificial distinction between investment income arising from the investment of policyholder funds and that arising from the investment of shareholder funds. Even in the case of mutual companies which are owned by their policyholders, the distinction is necessitated by the fact that last year's policyholder-owners may not be this year's policyholder-insureds.

When an insured purchases a policy of insurance, and pays for it up front, he or she suffers what is known as an *opportunity cost* by virtue of paying out the premium funds in advance of losses and expenses actually being paid. In theory, the policyholder could have invested the funds in some alternative until they were actually needed by the insurer. Where insurance rates are regulated for excessiveness, it is appropriate that this opportunity cost be recognized.

The opportunity cost should be calculated based upon the cash flows associated with the line of business, and should reflect the fact that not all cash flows go through invested assets - some portion being required for the infrastructure of the insurer. The buildings and desks and computer software which were originally purchased with someone else's premium dollars are now dedicated to providing service to current policyholders and should be viewed as being purchased at the beginning of the policy period and sold at the end.

Most importantly, the calculation should be made at a risk-free rate of return. It must be understood that the insured has not purchased shares in a mutual fund. The existence of an opportunity cost does not give the policyholder a claim on some part of the actual earnings of the insurer. Should the insurer engage in speculative investments resulting in the loss of policyholder supplied funds, the company cannot assess the insureds to make up the shortfall. By the same token, investment income over and above risk-free yields should not be credited to the policyholders in the ratemaking process.

Finally, investment income on surplus should be excluded from the ratemaking process. Policyholders' surplus represents owners' equity which is placed at risk in order to provide the opportunity for reward. While it provides protection to policyholders and claimants, the surplus does not **belong** to them. In fact, the inclusion of investment income on surplus creates a situation in which an insurer with a large surplus relative to premium must charge lower rates than an otherwise equivalent insurer with less surplus. In other words, lower cost for more protection. This, in my opinion, does not represent equitable or reasonable rate regulation.

One final distinction needs to be made. Rate regulation is generally a prospective process, and the methods and procedures recommended herein are designed to be efficacious on a prospective basis. When applied retrospectively, as in the case of excess profits regulations, it must be remembered that a single year of experience is rarely sufficient to assess the true profitability of a line of property and casualty business. In the case of low-frequency, high-severity lines such as earthquake, it may require scores, or even hundreds, of years to determine average profit on a retrospective basis.

RATEMAKING BASIS - NUMERICAL EXAMPLES

Consider a property and casualty insurer which writes only private passenger automobile insurance with the following expectations:

TABLE 1

PRIVATE PASSENGER AUTOMOBILE ASSUMPTIONS

(THOUSANDS OF DOLLARS)

Premium		$100,000
Loss Ratio		0.65
Expense Ratio		0.35
Loss Payout		
	Year 1	0.25
	Year 2	0.35
	Year 3	0.20
	Year 4	0.12
	Year 5	0.08

For purposes of this example, no distinction is made between pure losses and loss adjustment expenses. Premiums are assumed to be paid at policy inception, expenses at mid-term and losses at the midpoint of each year. Assume further that the risk-free rate of return is 6% per year and that 100% of underwriting cash flows are invested.

Shown below are the assumed cash flows along with the present value of those flows at 6% per year. The indicated profit—that is, the 6% present value of the underwriting cash flows—is $7,776 or 7.78% of premium.

TABLE 2

PRIVATE PASSENGER AUTOMOBILE RESULTS

(THOUSANDS)

Time	**Premium**	**Loss**	**Expense**	**Total Cash Flow**	**6.0% Present Value**
0.0	$100,000			$100,000	$100,000
0.5		$(16,250)	$(35,000)	(51,250)	(49,778)
1.5		(22,750)		(22,750)	(20,846)
2.5		(13,000)		(13,000)	(11,238)
3.5		(7,800)		(7,800)	(6,361)
4.5		(5,200)		(5,200)	(4,001)
Total	$100,000	$(65,000)	$(35,000)		$7,776

It is imperative that it be understood what this represents. This is the *a priori* expected net present value of the underwriting cash flows. It reflects the opportunity cost expected to be suffered by the average policyholder for the risk-free income lost through the advance payment of funds not yet required for infrastructure, loss payment or expense payment.

It is equally important to understand what this does not represent. It is not the money expected to be earned by the insurer from writing private passenger automobile insurance for one year. The insurer should expect to earn something greater than the risk-free rate of return in exchange for taking the risk that losses and expenses may exceed expectations. Nor is it the expected profit arising to owners for the year as it excludes funds generated from the investment of retained earnings and other income.

Note that this methodology is independent of level of surplus, actual investment results and past underwriting experience. It can be equitably applied to all companies and it is firmly grounded in both the substance of the insurance transaction and fundamental economic realities.

RATE-OF-RETURN—THE APPROPRIATE DENOMINATOR

As the examples above indicate, while it is fairly easy to calculate the dollar value of the *a priori* expected net present value of the underwriting cash flows associated with a given book of business under a given set of assumptions, the dollar value itself is of little value to a rate regulator charged with the assessment of whether proposed rates are inadequate or excessive.

Now it is imperative that we understand that it is the *rates* which are being regulated, not the rates-of-return. I am unaware of any rating law which states that "rates-of-return must not be excessive ..." Rate regulatory attention focused upon rate-of-return must be within the context of determination of what might constitute a reasonable profit loading in the rates, not as an attempt to equalize rates-of-return across insurers.

Two candidates for the denominator seem to be common - sales and equity. Assets might be an appropriate denominator from the standpoint of measuring economic efficiency, but equity is clearly the favorite of those seeking to measure relative values of investments while sales is favored by those who view profit provisions in the context of insurance rates themselves.

RETURN ON EQUITY

While there is little doubt that equity is an appropriate basis against which to measure company-wide financial performance of a property and casualty insurer, as I see it there are two basic problems with return-on-equity as a basis for measuring rate-of-return in rate regulation.

The first problem with return on equity is that it forces the regulator to forgo rate equity for rate-of-return equity.

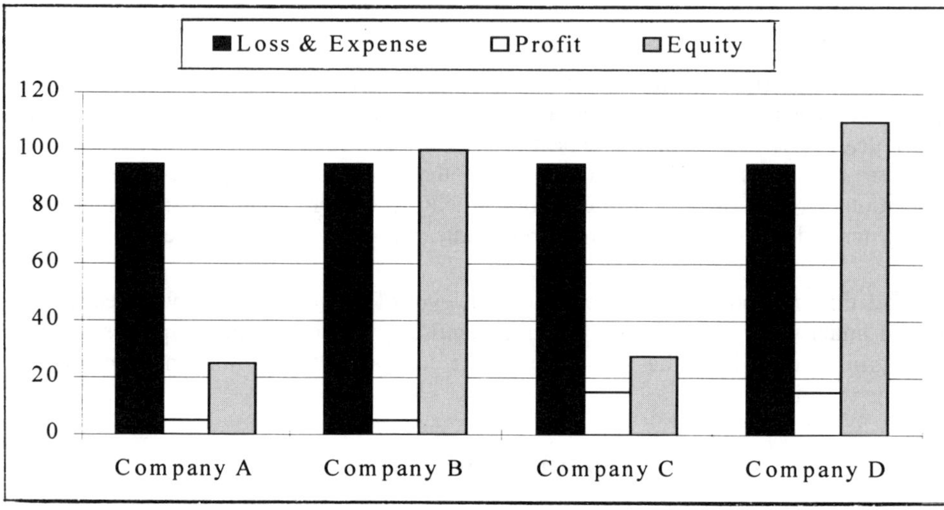

FIGURE 1. FOUR COMPANIES

Consider the example above. Here we have four companies, each writing the same coverage in the same market and providing the same level of service with an expected pure premium and expense component of $95. Companies A and B propose rates of $100 while companies C and D request approval of $110. Companies A and C are leveraged at a writings-to-surplus ratio of 4:1 while companies B and D are at 1:1.

The concept of rate equity would seem to require that companies A and B be treated identically as would C and D. But if we attempt to use equity as a base for rate-of-return this becomes a problem. Assume that the regulator has determined that a 15% return on equity is the appropriate benchmark for excessiveness. Our two highly-leveraged companies, A and C, project returns-on-equity of 20% and 55% respectively, while B and D are at 5% and 13.6%, respectively. If we use the return-on-equity benchmark we are forced to conclude that one $100 rate and one $110 rate should be disapproved as excessive while one $100 rate and one $110 rate are approved. We have subordinated rate equity to rate-of-return equity.

The second problem with return-on-equity in rate regulation is that it requires that equity be allocated to line of business and jurisdiction. And, no matter how much the rate-of-return advocate may wish to ignore the fact, there is no such thing as North Dakota Private Passenger Automobile Surplus - unless, of course, we are dealing with a company which writes North Dakota private passenger automobile insurance exclusively.

The fact is that the entire surplus of an insurer stands behind each and every risk. It supports all of the reserves related to all of the claims and policies issued by the company. And any artificial allocation of that surplus in no way limits the liability of the company to pay claims or honor other financial commitments.

By requiring the allocation of surplus to line and jurisdiction, the return-on-equity basis ignores the value inherent in unallocated surplus. In essence the method treats a multi-line national company with $100 million of surplus, $1 million of which is allocated to North Dakota private passenger automobile, identically with a North Dakota automobile insurer capitalized at $1 million. While the $99 million of "unallocated" surplus provides protection to the insured which would not be available from the small monoline insurer, this additional protection is assigned zero value where surplus is allocated.

There is also the problem of an equitable allocation basis. Just how should surplus be allocated to jurisdiction and line? How should the investment portfolio be assigned in order to track incremental gains and losses in allocated surplus? What do you do in the case of surplus exhaustion? Can any return be excessive when measured against an equity deficit? Or should the surplus simply be reallocated each year without regard to actual results? These are tough questions which must be answered by those seeking to allocate surplus.

"BENCHMARK" PREMIUM-TO-SURPLUS RATIOS AS A METHOD FOR SURPLUS ALLOCATION

Some regulators, when faced with the questions raised in the previous section, have proposed using average or target ratios of premium to surplus as "benchmarks" or "normative" ratios.

In the chart below, return on equity is assumed to be 12.5%. This corresponds to a return on sales of 25% where writings are 50% of surplus and 2.5% where the risk ratio is 5:1.

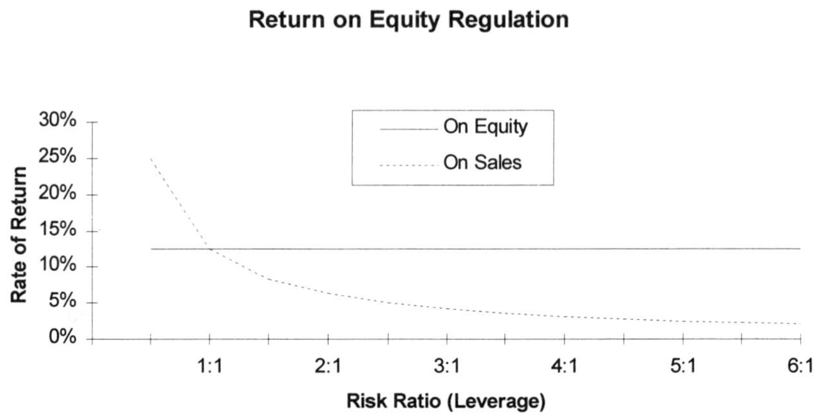

FIGURE 2

But what happens if we decide to use a benchmark risk ratio of 3:1 to allocate surplus to this particular line for this particular jurisdiction? As shown below, the return on equity will equal 12.5% only in the case where the risk ratio is actually 3:1. Where the risk ratio is lower, the return on equity will be lower. Where the risk ratio is above 3:1, the return on equity will exceed 12.5%.

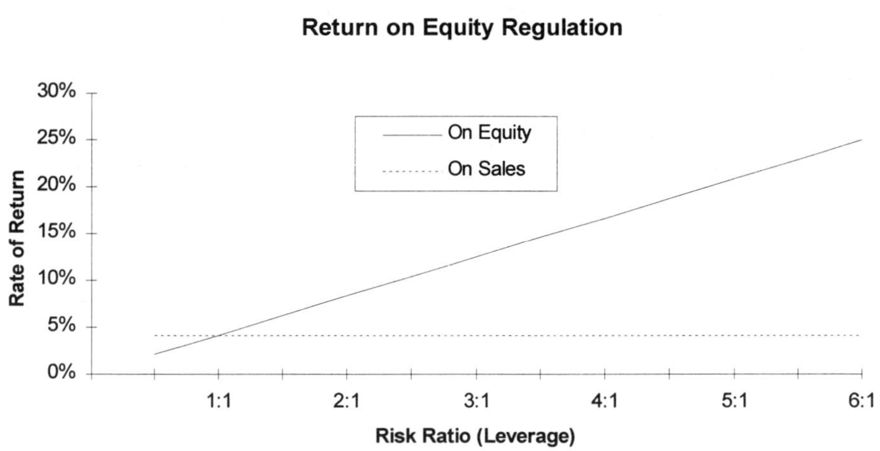

FIGURE 3

But the return on sales is now a constant (12.5%/3) = 4.1667% regardless of the actual risk ratio.

While the use of the benchmark writings-to-surplus ratio has eliminated the surplus allocation problem, the result is not return-on-equity regulation but return-on-sales regulation. And while there is nothing wrong with return-on-sales as a regulatory basis, this represents an excruciatingly complex method for return-on-sales regulation.

RETURN ON SALES

Return-on-sales relates the profit provision in the premium to the premium itself. For anyone who is familiar with the concept of *markup*, it is a natural way to view the profit component. It provides meaningful and useful information to the consumer. If you tell someone that 5% of the price of a loaf of bread represents profit to the grocer, that is helpful in the assessment of the "value" of the bread. If, on the other hand, you tell that someone that the price of the bread contains a 12.5% provision for return-on-equity to the grocer, the information is next-to-useless.

Return-on-sales based rate regulation is simply the establishment of benchmarks for what constitutes excessive or inadequate profit provisions as percentages of premium. It can be as simple as the 1921 NAIC Profit Formula which allowed 5% of premium for underwriting profit (and an additional 3% for conflagrations) or it can be as complicated as the use of benchmark writings-to-surplus ratios applied to permitted return-on-equity provisions. But however the allowable provisions are established, the application is premium-based, and independent of the relationship between premium and equity. As such, return-on-sales results in true rate regulation, not rate-of-return regulation.

PROFITABILITY STANDARDS

Whether rate-of-return is measured against sales or equity, the rate regulator must make a determination as to what constitutes a reasonable, not excessive, not inadequate, provision for profit in insurance rates. In order to keep the various components of the typical rate filing in perspective, I have prepared the following chart which represents an approximation of the composition of a typical private passenger automobile rate filing.

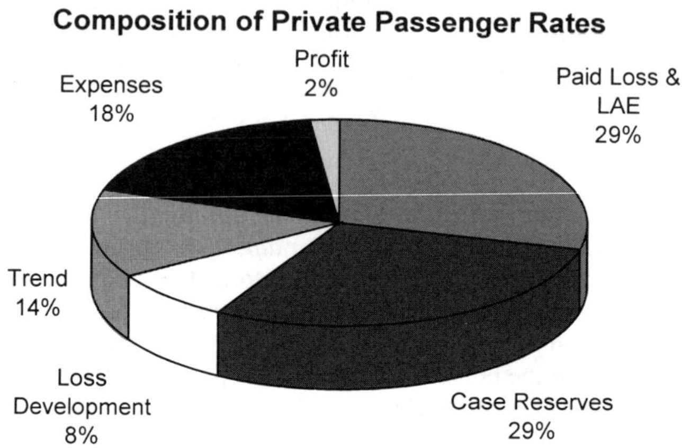

It is important to understand that there is typically a great deal of uncertainty in the calculation of indicated property and casualty insurance rates. In the private passenger example above, over 50% of the rate is comprised of estimated unpaid losses and trend. With a profit provision of approximately 2%, a small underestimation can eliminate the profit altogether. (On the other hand, a small overestimation can effectively double the profit.)

While the CAS *Statement of Principles Regarding Property and Casualty Insurance Ratemaking* states that "the underwriting profit and contingencies provisions are the amounts that, when considered with net investment and other income, provide an appropriate total after-tax return" there is no universally-accepted view of what constitutes an *appropriate* return. The application of rate regulatory authority in the U. S. evidences wide disparity. It is quite possible that a profit provision which might be viewed as excessive in one jurisdiction might be deemed inadequate in another.

There is, however, a relationship between the benchmark for excessiveness adopted within a jurisdiction and the resultant market conditions. Unlike public utilities, which are generally monopolistic and which have customer bases which are considerably more homogeneous than are insurance risks, property and casualty insurers can react to inadequate rates by tightening underwriting and/or reducing volume. In any given jurisdiction, the size and composition of the residual market, the number of insurers in the voluntary market, and the degree of product diversity and innovation are all related to the insurance industry perception of the opportunity to earn a reasonable return from the risk transfer.

Given the relationship between rate adequacy and market conditions, the proper benchmark for excessiveness for a regulator is that which will produce the desired market characteristics. And any regulator who believes that this relationship is less powerful than a well-crafted econometric argument for a given maximum profit provision is destined to learn a lesson about the distinction between theory and practice.

CONCLUSION

This discussion has focused on the measurement of profitability in the rate regulatory environment. It must be understood that insurance company management and owners will necessarily have different, and not necessarily consistent, needs when it comes to the measurement of profitability. Management will be primarily concerned with the relative risk and return expectations associated with alternative lines of business and jurisdictions. Shareholders will be more interested in returns relative to alternative investments while policyholder-owners of mutual companies will focus on premium savings and dividends. No single basis for the measurement of profitability will adequately meet the needs of all of these interests.

Where rate regulation is concerned, however, it is clear that there must be a consistent basis for the assessment of what constitutes excessiveness in a rate which can be equitably applied to all insurers and which will facilitate fair treatment of policyholders. Such a basis is the return-on-sales approach.

It has been alleged that actuaries have made a profession out of taking something simple and making it complex. While I certainly do not agree with that allegation, William of Ockham pointed out in the fourteenth century that simplicity is to be preferred over complexity. There are simple ways to measure profit and there are very complex ways. Similarly, there are complex ways to assess rate-of-return by jurisdiction and line of business and there are simple ways. Let us not assume that the complex ways are preferable solely because they are not simple.

CHAPTER NINE
THE CONFIRMED OPERATING RETURN APPROACH

by Judith Mintel

One approach to the regulation of insurance rates, and in particular the profit provision, which is by no means new but which is consistent with the developing legal principles in this area and also simple enough to be practical and fair in the rate regulatory context is the "Confirmed Operating Return" approach. It is an approach which encompasses both total return and operating return analyses.

The Confirmed Operating Return contemplates the development of a range of target operating returns expressed as a percentage of premium. The process of developing the range of target operating returns would first involve the selection of a range of total rates of return on net worth by reference to cost of capital or comparable industry returns analyses on an all-lines, all-states basis for a company group or, on an industry-wide basis for a particular line and state. This range of total returns can then be converted to a range of operating returns expressed as a percentage of premium. This process allows one to check or confirm the range of target operating returns for consistency with investor expectations on an overall basis and also allows a comparison with returns in other industries. However, in directly proposing or regulating the rates of any individual company, in any one state or line, the operating return range would be the one and only standard used.

The following illustration shows a typical conversion from a selected total rate of return of 15.5% of equity to an operating return of 5% of premium.

<u>Relationship of Insurance Profit Measures</u>

1)	Total Rate of Return (after tax) (% of GAAP Equity)	15.5%
2)	Ratio of GAAP Equity to Surplus	1.10
3)	Total Rate of Return (after tax) (% of Surplus)	17.0%
4)	Investment Income on Surplus (after tax)	7.0%
5)	Operating Return (after tax) (% of Surplus)	10.0%
6)	Leverage Ratio: Premium to Surplus	2 to 1
7)	Operating Return (after tax) (% of Premium)	5.0%

The total rate of return can be selected by any one of several methods, many of which are discussed in other chapters in this book. The ratio of GAAP Equity to Surplus, investment income on surplus, and the premium to surplus ratio can be selected by reference to industry practice and industry results. This conversion illustrates how an operating return of 5.0% of premium can be equivalent to a total rate of return of 15.5%.

Once a target total rate of return has been selected and the conversion from total rate of return to operating return has been accomplished, the resulting operating return can then be used to evaluate an individual insurer's rates in a particular line and a particular state. This process provides the necessary information to evaluate rates from a legal point of view.

The Confirmed Operating Return approach thus uses a total rate of return analysis but only at the proper level. A total return analysis is an appropriate basis for determining a target rate of return for owners of and investors in entire insurance company groups in comparison with the returns produced by companies in other industries that compete for investment capital. It is relevant to owners because it measures the return on the amount or the value of their investment. It is comparable to other industries because all are measured on a reasonably consistent basis. However, the returns for companies in other comparable industries are not usually broken down by division, by product line or geographical area, so in order to compare properly insurance industry returns to returns in other industries the appropriate level is the entire insurance company group or the entire insurance industry. The Confirmed Operating Return approach uses the information provided by a total return analysis in the most appropriate way possible while a similar analysis applied by individual company, by line, by state would not.

This Confirmed Operating Return approach also has significant benefits for use directly in rate regulation because the profit allowance can actually be used to adjust premiums while a rate of return on equity or net worth standing alone cannot. Insurance rates are developed by company, by line, by state and an operating return lends itself to these types of breakdowns whereas a total rate of return does not. Another important reason for the use of a Confirmed Operating Return in the rate regulatory process is that it does not create any counter-currents to solvency regulation in that it does not purport to regulate each individual insurer's actual premium-to-surplus ratio; it does not require arbitrary allocations of an insurer's surplus.

Thus, the Confirmed Operating Return is relatively simple and avoids many controversial issues.[1] At the same time, the range of operating returns selected does consider investment income on net worth because it was derived from an equivalent range of total

[1] One example of a controversial issue that should be mentioned is the treatment of capital gains, both realized and unrealized. To the extent that capital gains and losses are attributable to surplus rather than to returns on assets equivalent to insurance operations reserves, many of the controversial issues associated with this subject are avoided in the context of a rate hearing by using the confirmed operating return approach advocated here.

returns on net worth and its appropriateness has been confirmed by comparison to the total returns of other similar industries and investor expectations.

The Confirmed Operating Return approach is important from the legal perspective because it allows clear delineation to be made between an insurer's overall performance and the results of its insurance operations for a particular line and particular state. An operating loss using this measure means that the premiums paid by consumers in a particular line and state plus the investment income generated from those premiums is expected to be less than the claim costs and all other expenses (not including cost of capital) associated with the insurance coverage. In other words, a negative operating return means a company has not been allowed enough revenue to cover its out-of-pocket costs for that state and line. Any rate anticipating an operating loss necessarily means that investment earnings on capital put in place prior to the period of the rate must be used to guarantee performance.

If a court or other tribunal is presented with a total return analysis as the only measure of profit in an insurance rate case, no evidence is present that distinguishes between the successful operation of the insurance business and the investment results from past profits. The result is confusion and an inability to distinguish returns on the core insurance business from unrelated investment returns. A court cannot evaluate whether a company is operating successfully, whether a company is able to cover out-of-pocket expenses, or whether rates are inadequate pursuant to certain statutory and constitutional requirements without a way of differentiating between current insurance operations and investment returns on capital.

Investment income generated from an insurance company's capital or net worth must be separated for purposes of evaluating profit provisions by line, by state and by individual company in a group because capital plays a dual role for an insurer. An insurance company's capital is invested and produces an investment return whether or not the company actually issues any insurance policies. The investment returns generated by net worth are indicative of the degree of risk associated with the nature of those specific investments. An insurance company exposes capital (which remains invested) to additional risk by entering the business of insurance. This additional risk is that the capital may be called upon to satisfy claims and pay expenses if the insurance operation is unprofitable. If there is no return on insurance operations, there is no reason to remain in the insurance business, at least not in the state or line that produces no operating return.

How positive the insurance operating return must be is dependent upon the risk associated with the insurance business. Since there is some risk associated with the insurance business, the operating return must be positive at least to some degree. No insurer can operate successfully, maintain its financial integrity or attract capital and at the same time suffer operating losses. An operating loss means that an insurer's total returns were penalized because it entered the insurance business and placed its capital at risk in that business.

Any legal analysis of the insurance profit provision requires information concerning cost of capital, returns in other comparable industries and investor expectations, but evidence is also needed which separates profit on current insurance operations from investment returns on net worth or capital. The Confirmed Operating Return approach outlined above is an approach to establishing appropriate profit margins in property and casualty insurance rates that satisfies both legal requirements.

CHAPTER TEN
THE PROFIT PROVISION

by Charles F. Toney II

OVERVIEW

McClenahan and D'Arcy agree that profit should vary with the risk involved in transacting the business. The task is to estimate what profit is appropriate for a given level of risk. I shall address what I think are the characteristics of a proper risk-load, and I shall conclude with why I support the percentage of premium position at this time.

WHY DO WE CARE ABOUT THE PROFIT PROVISION?

When selecting a proper method for determining the profit provision, it helps to consider the context within which the profit provision is being used. Consider the following:

1. The actuary is given a goal from upper management that targets a certain return on either premium, equity, assets or any other base. If this is the context for which we are determining the profit provision for a rate, there is little controversy and less theory. We will set the rate level in such a way that the target return is expected to be earned.

2. The actuary bases the rate level on the current market conditions for a line of insurance in a given region. Again, there is little controversy and little theory involved. If the price is determined by market conditions, we do not need to be concerned with a theoretically appropriate profit provision.

3. The actuary wishes to determine the theoretically appropriate, risk-adjusted, profit provision. In this case, I am unaware of any method that adequately adjusts the required profit for all of the relevant risks involved. We need not go further since we do not have adequate tools.

4. The actuary wishes to determine a profit provision that will meet the requirements imposed by regulation. Obviously, the actuary must review the regulation and set the profit provision in such a way that it does not violate the regulatory standards. Again, theory does not matter. What matters is the standards set by the regulator.

5. The actuary is attempting to aid the regulators or management in determining the proper standard for a profit provision. I believe that this is the primary situation where any debate over a proper profit provision becomes useful. For regulators, the debate centers around a standard for rates that would not be excessive. For management, the debate centers on what would be the appropriate profit goals for this

portion of the company's operations. Realistically, these standards will not follow risk theory completely. Given that fact, an arbitrary return on sales standard is just as valid as an arbitrary return on equity standard or a discounted cash-flow analysis that uses an arbitrary discount rate.

THE PROPER RISK-LOAD FOR AN INSURANCE RATE

Consider the following companies. Assume the books of business are identical.

TABLE 1

	A	B
Surplus	$ 100,000,000	$ 50,000,000
Premium	100,000,000	100,000,000
Fixed Expense	20,000,000	20,000,000
Variable Expense	15%	15%
Investment Income	8,000,000	6,000,000
Losses	58,000,000	58,000,000
Profit	$ 15,000,000	$ 13,000,000
ROE	15%	26%

While the risk from transacting this business to both the policyholder and to the company is different given the surplus positions of each of the companies above, I know of no theory which would account for the magnitude of the difference in the proper theoretically required profit provision. Yet, economic principles state that in a competitive market, the price for a commodity should move towards an equilibrium and neither **A** nor **B** would be able to move this equilibrium price by itself. Property and casualty insurance is considered by many economists to have many of the characteristics of a competitive market.

Imagine the above two companies were given the option of transacting business in a new line that had the following characteristics:

TABLE 2

Expected Losses	$ 5,800,000
Expected Investment Income	$ 800,000
Fixed Expenses	$ 2,000,000
Variable Expenses	15%

Below are some questions that illustrate the difficulty of determining an appropriate profit provision:

1. Should **A** choose profit provision that would produce a 15% ROE and **B** choose a profit provision which would produce a 26% ROE? Or, should the premium and the profit provision be similar?

2. From a regulator's point of view, should the two programs have the same price, or should the price vary due to the ROE requirements?

3. From the policyholder's point of view, how much of a premium difference would be acceptable to compensate for the extra safety provided by **A**, which has double the surplus?

I believe that, given an accurate risk-load, all profit models would generate comparable results, whether the model is based on a percentage of sales, discounted cash flow analysis, return on equity, return on assets, etc. The differing results generated by the various models can partly be attributed to the lack of an accurate method for determining the proper risk-loading for a rate. A true risk-load should be a function of the following:

1. The variability of the existing book of business: It is generally accepted that the different insurance lines do not vary in a uniform way. The risk load for each company should reflect the expected variability of that company's mix of business. An accurate risk-load should reflect the unique and changing characteristics of the company's portfolio of business.

2. The variability of the line for which the rate is being made: It would be wrong to expect uniform variability from every line of insurance. A line, such as earthquake insurance, would not exhibit the same variability as automobile physical damage. Even within a given line of insurance, the expected variance will differ depending on factors such as the company's marketing strategy, the geographic distribution of the exposures, the limit or deductible profile, etc. A company having a large concentration of homeowners business in a relatively small geographic area would face greater risk, due to the exposure to a catastrophic loss, than another company with a widely distributed book of homeowners business, all else being equal.

3. The variability in the investment portfolio: Each company follows its own investment strategy. Some companies accept higher investment risk for the expectation of higher investment return. Since the investment strategy contributes to each company's ability to honor its obligations, it can be argued that the characteristics of the investment portfolio should contribute to the estimation of a proper risk-load.

4. The amount of surplus available to the company, especially relative to the variability of insurance and investment operations: The smaller the company's surplus, relative to its premium writings and its liabilities, the greater the risk that the company will be unable to meet its obligations. Economic theory states that shareholders should demand a higher expected rate of return for accepting the greater uncertainty in

results. This higher expected return would increase the total profit provision, but not necessarily through a risk-load provision. Note that the opposite is true for the policyholders. The policyholder should be willing to pay a premium for coverage from a company with a relatively secure surplus position. Policyholders should demand a discount from companies that are less stable financially.

5. The variability in the prospective investment market: Expected changes in the financial markets will affect the company's ability to meet its obligations. An interest rate assumption could be based, in part, on such expectations.

6. The impact the new policies or the new rate (possibly with a reduction in total policies) will have on the variability of the existing portfolio: A company's portfolio of insureds will change in response to a rate filing. If possible, the risk-load should reflect the expected variability of the portfolio after the rate change, rather than the variability of the company's historic or current portfolio.

7. Ideally, the change in variability of the portfolio attributable to any individual risk written at the new rate: Here, I am advocating a dynamic risk-load algorithm. I shall use earthquake insurance to illustrate my point. One hundred written exposures in a given geographic region will expose the company to some undefined level of risk. I shall call this level of riskiness X. The problem for developing a risk-load is that when the company's exposure increases to 1000, the riskiness increases to something greater than 10X. A dynamic risk-load is more appropriate for this coverage. Some commercially available earthquake insurance computer models attempt to do just that.

If there is no theory accurately reflects these considerations, what practical method can be used to determine the price? Three common methods are listed below.

I. Market price, possibly with a deviation.

   A. Evaluate the pricing of competitors.

   B. Profit analysis is limited to determining that a profit exists. For competing projects, choose the project with the highest profit relative to the estimated risk.

   C. Many companies' prices today are driven by market price analysis.

II. Return on Equity Analysis.

   A. One form would have the required ROE provided either by the regulator or by the upper management of the company. This form of ROE analysis ignores the risk-characteristics of the product being priced. Many companies set their rates in this manner.

B. A risk-based target ROE would be a more theoretically accurate method. Again, I know of no theory that considers all forms of risk.

C. In any ROE analysis, the allocation of equity is problematic.

III. Return on Sales.

A. This method is simple. In many industries, this is the method for determining a profit provision. Historically, this was the way a profit provision was determined. Many insurers continue to price this way.

B. This method, discounted cash-flow analysis, and ROE should be equivalent if consistent assumptions are used in formulating the risk-load.

C. If the methods are equivalent, why not use the simpler one?

CONCLUSION

Since I believe that there is no accepted theory for determining a proper risk-loading, and since the allocation of equity for a ROE analysis is problematic, I feel that there are two simple and acceptable ways to set a rate. The first would be to determine the level of rates in the market, and setting the prospective rates based on this market analysis. In a truly competitive market, this method would be required.

To the extent that insurance is not a commodity, and to the extent that the insurance marketplace violates some of the economic assumptions underlying the theory of competitive markets, the determination of a profit provision becomes more meaningful. I believe that any profit provision can be, at best, an estimate of a theoretically sound quantity. Without an accurate method for determining the risk-loading, I feel that this estimate will be based on simplifications and assumptions. The result of such a formula may be accurate on average, and may even be unbiased. However, I feel that any such risk-load will not reflect the unique risks of the line being priced. If this is true, why not use a simple method for estimating the profit provision?

The return on sales method makes comparison with other companies relatively simple, and changes in target profits are easily transformed into rates. All things considered, I think that determining a profit provision as a percentage of sales is the most practical of the method available today.

CHAPTER ELEVEN

THE COST OF CAPITAL AN AXIOMATIC APPROACH

By Oakley E. Van Slyke, FCAS, ASA, MAAA

OVERVIEW

The Ratemaking Principles of the Casualty Actuarial Society include the following:

> Principle 2: A rate provides for all costs associated with the transfer of risk….
>
> The rate should include a charge for the risk of random variation from the expected costs. This risk charge should be reflected in the determination of the appropriate total return consistent with the cost of capital and, therefore, influences the underwriting profit provision.

This chapter describes a way to estimate the cost of risk using data from the capital markets. We approach the problem from a business perspective as well as an economic perspective. We conclude that both perspectives lead to the same conclusion, that the cost of risk is a property of the exposure being insured, and hence can be valued directly as a percentage of the premium per unit of exposure. Once estimated in this way, the result may be expressed in terms of an imputed allocation of capital and an imputed rate of return on capital, but the cost of capital must be found from the exposure first.

Calculating the risk charge requires a description of the scenarios that lead to unexpected levels of profit or loss as well as a description of the random components of individual claims. The risk charge is a function of the broad capital markets. The same approach to calculating risk charges can be applied to financial undertakings of all kinds. When covariance with the market is minimal, the market behaves as if there were a single parameter for the risk charge. When covariance with the market is significant, it can be accommodated by adding a second parameter to the description of the capital markets.

This approach is consistent with regulation, with business practice, and with general models of economic behavior. The calculations can be put in simple spreadsheets prepared by statistical agencies and individual companies. The regulation of premium rates is simplified dramatically because the cost of capital is simply a charge per unit of exposure or a fraction of expected losses, like loss adjustment expense. The cost of real reinsurance is clearly chargeable in ratemaking because it reduces the cost of capital so much that the indicated premium rate is lower when real reinsurance is present.

A BUSINESS PERSPECTIVE

Capital has many uses. In the typical insurance transaction, most of the value of capital comes from its role in supporting the assumption of risk. As Kreps points out in Chapter 6, surplus creates capacity to bear risk, and insuring risk uses up capacity. Other uses of capital, such as rewarding entrepreneurial innovation, have a small role, if any, in insurance pricing, and insurance regulators generally have no reason to include the value of such a role in the profit provision in regulated rates.

Clearly the prices of securities in the capital markets reflect a cost of capital. If a corporation with an A rating for its debt wishes to issues bonds, it will pay a premium compared to a corporation with an AAA rating. That premium is reflected in the lower selling price for its bonds, all else equal. Bond prices vary from industry to industry, and from company to company, to reflect the risk that the coupons and principle may not be paid.

This view of the cost of capital is similar to that voiced by Justice Douglas in the Hope Natural Gas case: "…the return to the equity owner should be commensurate with returns on investments in other enterprises having corresponding risks." (Mintel, Chapter 1). As Mintel points out, "…the language used by the Supreme Court seems to require an analysis that evaluates the riskiness of the business, an ability to compare returns among different industries and a method for determining a return…."

From 1921 to about 1970, profit and contingencies in property and casualty insurance rates were generally provided for by a provision for underwriting profit of a few percent; investment income was also allowed to accrue to the insurer. Michelbacher and Roos wrote in 1970 that a "provision must be included in the rates for profit, contingencies, and catastrophes."[1] In fire insurance, the National Association of Insurance Commissioners (NAIC) recommended an underwriting profit provision of 3% from 1921 to 1949.[2] This rule worked reasonably well because short-tailed lines of insurance had a lower cost of capital and the difference between the present value of the losses and the undiscounted value of the losses was a reasonable reward for the extra risk present in long-tailed lines of business.

In the 1970's the investment yields of property-casualty insurance companies were significantly greater than the yields that had prevailed in the previous fifty years. Although the rough approximations of the NAIC's profit provision had been criticized for many years, they were simply untenable during periods of high investment yields and unexceptional risks. While in retrospect it is difficult to see why the methods used successfully in the life insurance sector were not widely adopted, the fact is they were not. Several approaches were tried, but the major changes came about because of the

[1] MICHELBACHER AND ROOS (1970), p. 23.

[2] MICHELBACHER AND ROOS (1970), loc. cit.

automobile rate hearings in Massachusetts beginning in May, 1975.[3] During these hearings, investment income was specifically included in the ratemaking formula for regulated property-casualty insurance for the first time. The methods used were those of "Modern Financial Theory" and, in particular, the Capital Asset Pricing Model.[4]

Unfortunately, application of the Capital Asset Pricing Model generally degenerated into litigation about "the total financial need of the insurer" and how "the investment income expected to be earned" was to be measured.[5] These questions ran aground on the rocky shores of practical issues, such as:

> If no time elapsed between the date of issue and the date of loss, would there be a cost of capital? If fire insurance and liability insurance have the same risk profile, why would the time delay for the payment of liability claims affect the cost of capital?
>
> If claim payments are due, say, five years from the date of policy issue, does an increase in uncertainty about payments make the premium rate go up or down? If uncertainty makes premiums go up, does this mean there can be "negative discount rates" for insurance?
>
> If an insurance policy's results are uncorrelated with the performance of broad stock market indices, does the policy have no cost of capital? If an insurance policy's results are negatively correlated with the performance of broad stock market indices, does the policy have a negative cost of capital?

The issues underlying these questions are not implied by the Hope Natural Gas case. That case leaves in place the idea that the cost of capital is a function of the risks that are underwritten. It does not introduce the idea that the capital structure of the insurance company affects the cost of capital. It does not introduce the idea that retrospective measures of investment income play a role in ratemaking.

These questions make it clear that there is a fundamental difference between the time value of money (e.g., the present value of $1 deferred but certain) and the cost of risk. It would be far more practical, if it were correct to do so, to have the rate-maker calculate the cost of risk per unit of exposure and the time value of money at the time he or she calculates the expected losses per unit of exposure and their payment pattern. Even the use of judgment to estimate the cost of risk in a rate filing would be preferable to the use of a methodology that introduces inappropriate issues and historical information.

This business view is supported by economic theory.

---

[3] CUMMINS AND HARRINGTON (1987), p xiii and 120.

[4] Op. cit., p. 1

[5] MINTEL (1983), p. 186

AN ECONOMIC PERSPECTIVE

From an economic perspective, a cost is estimated to be the price that creates an equilibrium between supply and demand. The cost of capital in an insurance transaction is the equilibrium price in the capital markets for the use of capital to bear risk. Fortunately, this equilibrium price can be estimated using data from the capital markets.

One would have expected the question to be addressed from the 1950's on by the methods that economists successfully used to model the prices of other goods and services after ARROW and DEBREU (1954). Unfortunately, that approach had stalled in the 1960's. Here is Borch's summary of the development as of 1962:

> 1.1 The Walras-Cassel system of equations which determines a static equilibrium in a competitive economy is certainly one of the most beautiful constructions in mathematical economics. The mathematical rigour which was lacking when the system was first presented has since been provided by Wald (1936) and Arrow and Debreu (1954). For more than a generation one of the favourite occupations of economists has been to generalize the system to dynamic economies. The mere volume of the literature dealing with this subject gives ample evidence of its popularity.
>
> 1.2 The present paper investigates the possibilities of generalizing the Walras-Cassel model in another direction. The model as presented by its authors assumes complete certainty, in the sense that all consumers and producers know exactly what will be the outcome of their actions. It will obviously be of interest to extend the model to markets where decisions are made under uncertainty as to what the outcome will be. This problem seems to have been studied systematically only by Allais (1953) and Arrow (1953) and to some extent by Debreu (1959) who includes uncertainty in the last chapter of his recent book. It is surprising that a problem of such obvious and fundamental importance to economic theory has not received more attention. Allais ascribes this neglect of the subject to *son extrême difficulté*....
>
> 3.7 The problem on the *supply* side of a reinsurance market thus appears to be similar to the problems of maximization under restraints which occur in some production models. It is clear the problem will have a solution, at least under certain conditions.
>
> 3.8 The problems on the *demand* side are more complicated.[6]

The work of Wald, Arrow and Debreu, then, building on the Walras-Cassel equations, shows how to build a model of the equilibrium price of anything traded in a competitive

[6] BORCH (1962), p. 424, 431.

market. One begins with a model of the decisions facing the buyer and seller. One then determines the equations describing Pareto-optimal behavior. These are the supply and demand schedules that underlie equilibrium prices.

Parallel to the work of Arrow, Debreu, and Borch, practical economists in the United States had begun to employ the Efficient Market Principle as a sort of Ockham's razor to compare theory with data. The Efficient Market Principle states that the prevailing prices reflect *all* of the information available to the players in the market. Here is Stephen A. Ross addressing the Society of Actuaries in April, 1994:

> I actually trace the roots of the modern subject [of finance] back a bit further. I traced it to a wonderful, somewhat neglected article in 1937 by Cowles, who examined what we now call the efficiency of markets.... Efficient market theory lay dormant after Cowles until around the 1950s, and then it picked up steam in the 1960s and 1970s. It is the empirical basis for what we think of as modern finance. If you look closely, lurking in the background of option-pricing theory, asset-pricing models, and all of the paraphernalia of modern finance, are the fundamental intuitions of efficient market theory.... [T]he thought was that the current price was really some sense of the reflection of the consensus of all of the participants in the market. As such, it incorporates all of the information that people have.[7]

The Efficient Market Principle has been found to explain movements in prices in many markets. It is reasonable to expect any regulatory or management standards for ratemaking to reflect the Efficient Market Principle.

We begin by identifying the price behavior of insurance companies and other risk-taking firms. This is established in terms of equations of price if every firm is pursuing its Pareto-optimal price strategy. Specifically, every insurance company seeks to maximize its economic value. First we set out assumptions that are intuitive enough to be considered axioms.

THE AXIOMS

The axioms that underlie this approach to calculating the cost of capital are set out in Table 1. This list has been abridged slightly from the list in VAN SLYKE (1995).

The first three axioms are restatements of the axioms underlying Borch's theorem regarding risk transfers (BORCH (1962) and GERBER (1979)). Axiom 4 introduces the time value of money in the absence of risk. Asymptotically, as the amount of risk in a multi-period transaction diminishes toward zero, the cost of capital arising from the transfer of risk approaches that of a series of payments certain in the currency in which the transaction is denominated. Axiom 5 is the Efficient Market Principle.

---

[7] ROSS (1994), p. 1-2.

TABLE 1

THE AXIOMS

1. The players are averse to risk.
2. No player would pay \$X or more than \$X to be rid of a chance of losing \$X.
3. The price of capital for the use of underwriting risk is not unduly sensitive to small changes in the descriptions of the risks that are being transferred. By "description" we mean the forecasts of cash flows under a range of scenarios, their probabilities, and their timing.
4. If there is no risk but the outcomes result in flows of currency at future times, the time value of money can be determined from the current prices of risk-free bonds.
5. In the aggregate, prices reflect all of the information available to the players.
6. No individual buyer or seller controls the cost of capital.

Axioms **4** and **5** have the effect of creating a distinction between the time value of money and the cost of risk. The time value of money has to do with the ways governments print money, finance one another's economies, and the like. The time value of money is recognized explicitly by replacing all outcomes that may be realized at future times with their equivalent values in current dollars.

COMPUTATIONS OF THE COST OF RISK

Just as the prevailing price level of real estate determines the cost of real estate to the insurance company, the prevailing price level of capital in risk-taking transactions determines the cost of capital for ratemaking purposes.

These axioms imply that the cost of risk can be found from the simultaneous solution of the following three equations:

$$\pi = E[x] - P[x]$$

$$E[x] = \sum_k \sum_j \sum_i p(k)\, p\left(x = x_i \middle| t = t_j, k\right) x_i v_{t_j}$$

$$P[x] = -\frac{\pi}{s} \ln \sum_k p(k) \exp\left[-\frac{s}{\pi} \sum_j -\frac{\pi}{s} \ln \sum_i p\left(x = x_i \middle| t = t_j, k\right) e^{-s\frac{x_i v_{t_j}}{\pi}} \right]$$

These can be read, "The risk premium, or cost of risk, is the difference between the expected present value of the cash flows and the market price of the cash flows in light of the market's aversion to risk. The expected present value is the sum, over all possible amounts of cash flow, over all periods of time, over all possible scenarios, of the cash flows, weighted by their probabilities and present value factors reflecting the value of a dollar certain to be paid at time t_j. The market price of the cash flows is the weighted average of the present values of the cash flows, with each cash amount adjusted by scaling it by the risk premium and the risk-free present value factor, exponentiating it to give additional weight to adverse outcomes; when the weighted average has been computed, the exponentiation and dollar scaling are undone to get the result in dollars. The dollars over time within a scenario are offset against one another. The resulting present values for the scenarios are adjusted for the uncertainty among the scenarios." [8]

In the absence of risk, π is zero. If a set of transactions were listed from riskiest to least risky, the value of π would decrease as one moved down the list.

SCENARIOS

The concept of scenarios is crucial. In the equations above, the scenarios are denoted by the subscript k. Each scenario is defined by a set of assumptions about the ways outcomes are linked over time. For example, there might be a high litigation scenario, a high medical inflation scenario, or a high storm frequency scenario. Within each scenario, the probabilities of outcomes are independent of the outcomes at previous times. (Technically speaking, the outcomes are conditionally independent, conditioned on the occurrence of the particular scenario.) Within each scenario, income items in one time period offset outgo items in other time periods. Within an adverse scenario, the total effect of a series of costly years is added together to reflect the large amount of capital required to support the possibility of such a scenario. These sums across time periods within specific scenarios are done in dollars, not exponentiated units.

Often there is either random fluctuation or parameter uncertainty within a given scenario. The innermost sum accounts for variation given the assumptions of the particular scenario. In practice, it is sometimes more practical to explore a large number of deterministic scenarios and put all of the uncertainty in the between-scenario risk. When this is done, the equations simplify, and there is no sum over i. In other cases, such as for fire insurance, the risk might reasonably be represented by a single scenario, a single time, and a probability distribution of outcomes. In this case, the sums over j and k fall away, and the only sum is over i.

POOLING OF RISKS, LIMITATIONS ON LEVERAGE, AND REGULATION

These equations are "scaleable"; that is, if there are twice as many units of exposure, the three values $E[x]$, $P[x]$, and π all double in value. For example, if two reinsurance companies reinsure 10 million car-years and 20 million car-years, respectively, of a quota share contract, the premium received for the larger share will be twice the premium of the

[8] John Cozzolino has named the quantity *P[x]* the "Risk-Adjusted Value" of the cash flows. The term "economic value" has become more popular, at least in the context of management information systems. Stern Stewart & Co. has registered the service mark "EVA" to refer to its consultancy in "*Economic Value Added*". The Coca-Cola company featured a lengthy description of EVA in its 1995 annual report. See also "The Real Key to Creating Wealth" by Shawn Tully, Fortune, September 20, 1993.

smaller share. The equations are scaleable because they reflect the cost if the company must go to the capital markets to get the capital to underwrite the risk.

To the company writing many identical risks, however, the risks of individual policies are not scaleable. There is a decided advantage to risk pooling and a decided cost to excessive leverage. Although the cost of capital—in the capital markets—for underwriting \$100 million of automobile insurance premium in a year depends on the exposures and not on the capital structure of the company, for the company the marginal cost of capital might be more or less than the market average. Specifically, to the extent that the results on the \$100 million of automobile insurance are independent of the company's other financial results, the company will enjoy the benefit of risk pooling. Its marginal cost of capital will be less than indicated by the equations. On the other hand, to the extent that the results on the \$100 million of automobile insurance are positively correlated with the company's other financial results, the company will have a higher cost of capital than indicated by the equations. Its marginal cost of capital will suffer from the high leverage.

As a result, rate regulation based on a cost-of-capital formula that does not depend on which company retains the risk would lead companies to manage their leverage. This is a desirable outcome. On the other hand, requiring the cost of capital to vary to offset the effects of pooling and leverage would lead companies to employ excessive leverage or inadequate risk pooling compared to the equilibrium free-market situation. The result would be unnecessarily high premiums.

NUMERICAL EXAMPLES

It is easy to see the equations in terms of a spreadsheet to calculate the cost of risk. One simply puts in a list of possible net (after-tax, present-value) cash flows, associates a probability with each, estimates a value of s from market data, sets up the three equations, and runs the solver routine to find π. The hard work is to estimate the probabilities of the possible cash flows, but that must be done in any calculation of the cost of capital.

Table 2 shows the computation of the cost of a single unit of risk, which is defined, for these examples, to be the risk in one chance in 100 of losing \$1,000. This table includes a premium of \$100, which does not affect the value of the cost of risk but makes the illustration clearer. The cost of risk of \$116 per unit is the amount that satisfies the three equations above when the capital markets show a value of the parameter s of 0.50.

TABLE 2

CALCULATION OF THE COST OF ONE UNIT OF RISK

Market value of *s*	0.50		
Premium	126		
Loss	-1,000		
Event	Amount	Probability	Expected Value
Premium, then loss	-874	0.010	-9
Premium, no loss	126	0.990	125
			116
Economic Value			0
Expected Value			116
Cost of Risk			116

STONE (1973) examined several hypothetical insurance contracts. These were simple binomial risks that Stone developed to illustrate the basic principles.[9] Stone described a situation in which there were 2,000 identical bridges with parameters *p, L,* and *P*, each subject only to total loss, like this:

FIGURE 1

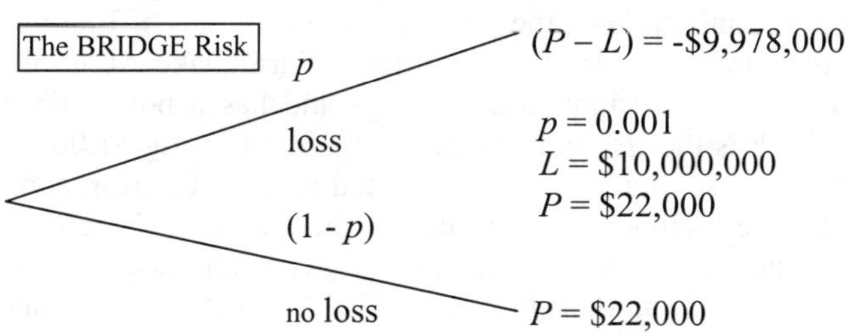

This premium of $22,000, while illustrative, is a realistic figure. If the capital markets were asked to absorb a single bridge risk like this, without any pooling, the price in the capital markets would be something like $750,000. This can be illustrated by applying the three equations to this problem. This is illustrated in Table 3.

---

[9] I am indebted to John Cozzolino for pointing out Stone's important work.

TABLE 3

COST OF RISK FOR STONE'S BRIDGE EXAMPLE

Market value of s	0.50		
Premium	780,067		
Loss	-10,000,000		
Event	Amount	Probability	Expected Value
Premium, then loss	-9,219,933	0.001	-9,220
Premium, no loss	780,067	0.999	779,287
			770,067
Economic Value			0
Expected Value			770,067
Cost of Risk			770,067

Here the economic value is zero because at the premium of $780,067 the company is indifferent about underwriting the bridge contract. On the other hand, if a single insurer were to take a portfolio of 2,000 such risks to the market, the premium per bridge would be only about $13,000, less than that cited in Stone's example. The importance of pooling is discussed at length below.

RUSSO AND VAN SLYKE (1996) applied these equations to two dramatically different transactions in the capital markets, the purchase of $2 million of Baa bonds in the bond market, and the reinsurance layer of the California Earthquake Authority (CEA), which attaches at $4 billion plus accumulated earnings and has a policy limit of $2 billion. Again, the unit of risk is the risk in one chance in 100 of losing $1,000. The results are shown in Figure 2. Russo and Van Slyke reported values of s from about 0.35 to about 0.55 depending on the assumptions they used; this variation is reflected in Figure 2. While much empirical work remains to be done to get a full understanding of the market parameter s, it seems clear that its value is such that the cost of risk in one chance in 100 of losing $1,000 is about $100, not $30 or $40.

FIGURE 2

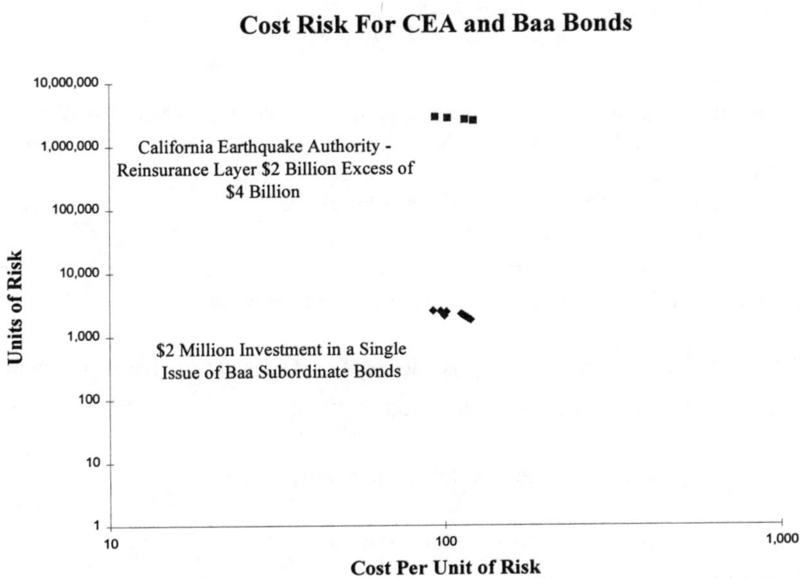

It is striking that two transactions in such widely different parts of the world-wide capital markets displayed such similar values for the cost per unit of risk. The data could have indicated two different costs per unit of risk, say $50 and $150. The data did not. This consistency in the cost per unit of risk is a result of the data, not an illusion created by the model.

The Efficient Market Principle suggests that this will be the case. Investors can invest in Baa bonds or in the stock of reinsurance companies, as well as many other investments, and they adjust their investments to reflect their expectations of risk. If there were a greater price for underwriting risk in one part of the capital market, capital would flow into that part, driving up the supply, and driving down the price.

It is precisely these estimates of the cost of risk that should be used in ratemaking.

RATEMAKING

For ratemaking purposes, these equations can be applied to the losses, while premiums and expenses can be considered separately.

The expression for the expected present value of losses can be restated in terms of the "duration" of losses and the risk-free interest rate.

$$E[x] = E[L]\{1 - D_m r_f\}$$

That is, the expected present value of the losses is the undiscounted expected value of the losses, diminished by the adjusted MacCauley duration times the risk-free rate of interest. This is an approximation, but it is adequate. There are second-order expressions for duration, but their accuracy is not necessary for ratemaking.

The net cost to the insurer to underwrite *N* policies with *M* total units of exposure at premium rate *P* and total premium *PM* is the sum of the following costs:

$ME[L]\{1 - D_m r_f\}$ where *E[L]* is the expected loss rate per unit of exposure, without discount for risk or the time value of money

$M\pi$ where π is the average cost of risk per policy

$M\,U_M$ where U_M denotes those underwriting expenses that increase with the number of units of exposure

$N\,U_N$ where U_N denotes those underwriting expenses that increase with the number of policies

$P\,U_P$ where U_P denotes those underwriting expenses that increase with the policy premium *P*

$P\,C$ where *C* is the commission rate

$P\,T$ where *T* is the premium tax rate

The premium equation becomes:

$$P = \frac{E[L]\{1 - D_m r_f\} + \pi + U_M + \dfrac{N}{M}U_N}{1 - (U_P + C + T)}$$

This can be read, "The premium rate per unit of exposure is the total fixed cost per unit of exposure divided by the complement of the costs that vary with premium. The total fixed cost per unit of exposure is the expected present value of the losses at the risk-free rate of return, plus the cost of risk, plus the underwriting expenses per unit of exposure."

Today the rating bureaus and larger companies publish the values of expected losses. Determining these values requires the analysts to forecast the loss payments over time. Also, the forecasts are uncertain, and the uncertainty can be estimated from the assumptions and data used to forecast the losses. From this data the rate-maker can compute the MacCauley duration and the average cost of capital per unit of exposure. Either the rate-maker or the regulator can publish the risk-free interest rate to be used for each duration; it can easily be read from the trading prices of U. S. Treasury securities on any day.

Forecasts of undiscounted losses and arcane discussions about the appropriateness of profit should be replaced with explicit calculations of the present value of losses and the cost of capital. All of this seems remarkably out-of-step with the "Modern Theory of Finance" only because of the customs that have arisen around discussions of investment portfolios, which make it difficult to discuss the cost of capital in the way we do here. These customs are not based on an economic analysis of equilibrium prices in capital markets.

Application of the equations to determine the cost of risk, π, requires a careful description of the risks of underwriting the insurance. It does **not** require that one step in the calculation is an allocation of surplus or assets to the particular block of insurance. Of course, once one has calculated the cost of risk π to be a certain number of dollars per unit of exposure, that result can be *expressed* as a certain return on a certain amount of imputed surplus. This is merely a way of describing the cost, not a way of estimating it.

In this formulation, the capital structure of the insurance company is not relevant in determining the premium rate. There is no need to allocate capital or surplus among lines and sub-lines. Sound companies command the same premium whether they are using their capital fully or not. They have the same cost of risk when they look to the capital markets to support their underwriting.

REINSURANCE

The cost of capital is ultimately determined by the cost of the worst risks, unless they are remote. Care must be taken to identify the worst scenarios and establish realistic probabilities for those scenarios. The estimates of probabilities should be based on historical data to the extent possible. Ratemaking, determining policy terms, and risk management all go hand in hand.

Reinsurance increases the expected cost of losses and expenses by introducing the transaction costs and profit margins of the reinsurer. Reinsurance that transfers significant risk lowers the expected total of losses, expenses, and the cost of capital, however. This beneficial effect of reinsurance should be reflected in rate filings. Especially when reinsurance is effectively essential to the prudent underwriting of risks, as is typically the case for homeowners insurance, the costs of reinsurance should be reflected in the premium rates, along with the lower value of the cost of capital that is the result of the reinsurance.

Table 4 shows the cost of risk and total premium for a 50% share of two of Stone's bridge policies.

TABLE 4

COST OF RISK FOR 50% SHARE OF TWO BRIDGE POLICIES

Market value of *s*	0.50		
Premium	450,303		
Size of Each Loss	-5,000,000		
Event	Amount	Probability	Expected Value
Premium, then one loss	-4,549,697	0.0019980	-9,090
Premium, then two losses	-9,549,697	0.0000010	-10
Premium, no loss	450,303	0.9980010	449,403
			440,303
Economic Value			0
Expected Value			440,303
Cost of Risk			440,303

In this example, the cost of risk has been reduced from \$770,067 to \$440,303 even though the expected value of loss payments is unchanged. This reduction in the cost of risk has reduced the total premium from \$780,067 to \$450,303. By extending this to a Poisson process for 2,000 identical bridge contracts, the estimated premium per bridge is just \$13,951, and the total risk premium for 2,000 bridges is \$7.9 million.

Indicated premium rates will be lowest if sound reinsurance is recognized. When reinsurance does not transfer real risk, as in some window-dressing contracts, the regulator might disallow its costs. The company might reasonably be asked to justify any provisions for reinsurance that do not minimize the economic cost to the primary insurer. Except in these unusual situations, the cost of reinsurance is a legitimate insurance company expense.

EXPOSURE IN RATEMAKING

Although characterized in rate hearings as a debate between a Return on Equity school and a Return on Premium school, the real debate is about whether the measure of exposure alone can accurately capture the information about the cost of capital. Ratemaking based on exposure may reflect the particular losses and exposures of the insurer selling the insurance, but otherwise it does not depend on the firm selling the insurance.

An appropriate measure of exposure is, of course, proportional to the expected level of loss costs. As noted above, the expected present value of losses, $E[x]$, the economic value of the losses, $P[x]$, and the risk premium π are all scaleable. That is, they all change in tandem with across-the-board changes in the cash flows denoted by x. Therefore, the cost of risk is a fixed proportion of the losses.

The proportion depends on the uncertainty of the cash flows and their distribution over time. The proportion therefore varies from one kind of insurance to the next. On the other hand, the cost of risk as a proportion of expected losses does not vary among insurance companies except to the limited extent the individual insurer's operations change the probabilities of loss payments or their timing.

(The proportion also depends on the capital market's valuations of risk-free securities and the capital market's aversion to risk, both of which can be determined without reference to the ratemaking problem at hand and introduced into the ratemaking procedure as external constants at the time the rates are promulgated.)

The cost of risk is therefore a fixed amount per unit of exposure. The fixed amount depends on the forecasts of loss payments, including their timing and estimates of the possible payments and their probabilities. The cost of risk is a function only of ratemaking data, the risk-free rate of return, and the capital market's cost per unit of risk as embodied in the parameter s which determines the market's price per unit of risk.

Finally, the reduction in the cost of risk per unit exposure brought about by the pooling of many units of exposure should be reflected in the computation by applying the formulas to the volume of exposures being underwritten. For personal lines ratemaking, most of the risk in the policies subject to a given rate filing arises from parameter uncertainty or the risk of conflagration or windstorm. For personal lines, therefore, the average cost of risk per unit of risk will not vary significantly whether the loss forecasts encompass $100 million of losses or $1 billion. The cost of risk per unit of exposure is the cost of risk for the insured exposures of a representative firm divided by the number of units of exposure.

COVARIANCE WITH THE MARKET

ROSS (1976) had the great insight that risks whose outcomes are independent of the outcomes of the broad capital markets should command a lower cost of capital than risks that have outcomes that are positively correlated with the movements of broad market averages. For example, an investment that performs well when the economy is strong and performs poorly when the economy is weak is less valuable than a risk whose expected outcomes move in the opposite way.

As Ross shows, the cost of capital can be expected to vary with the relationship of the risk's outcomes to a number of factors in the broad portfolio of risks in the capital market. Ross suggested the use of factor analysis to find the relationship of the cost of capital for a particular risk to a composite market factor. Factor analysis is a statistical procedure that identifies a set of constants to apply to a number of independent variables to create a composite variable that best explains the performance of an independent variable. Adopting this idea, a composite variable could be found that has the property that the market's cost per unit of risk is a linear function of that composite variable. The results would be like those shown in Figure 3.

FIGURE 3

THE CAPITAL MARKET LINE

THE COST OF RISK PER UNIT OF RISK AS A FUNCTION OF MARKET

(Illustrative example)

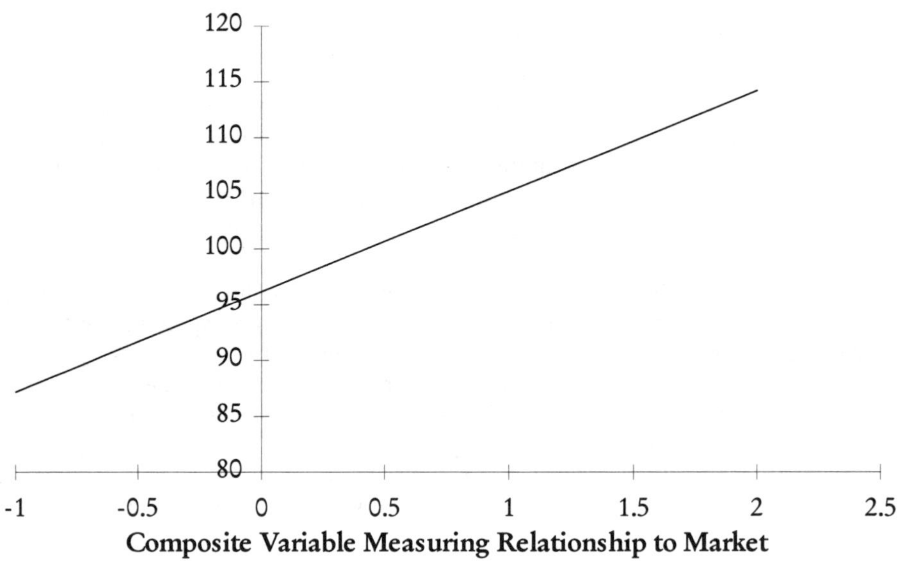

Thus, the Beta of the Capital Asset Pricing Model is replaced by a composite economic indicator particular to the risk. Risks whose outcomes move in tandem with broad market averages command a higher cost per unit of risk than risks whose outcomes are independent of broad market averages.

Note that this is contrary to the key conclusion of the Capital Asset Pricing Model that risks that are *independent* of the market have *no* cost of risk. That conclusion is a result of certain assumptions of the Capital Asset Pricing Model that do not apply in general.

Most property-casualty risks are not significantly correlated with the outcomes of the capital markets as a whole. The value of π per unit of risk can be assumed to be a constant for rate regulation purposes except for such lines as surety, which usually are not regulated.

COMPARISON TO PRACTICE

Most goods and services in most industries are priced using mark-ups that are a percentage of sales. Return-on-sales rules may not be unique to the insurance world, but return-on-investment rules are unique to the investment world.

In most jurisdictions, in most lines of property-casualty insurance, the price of insurance is set by the competitive market, either with or without the prior approval of filed rates. In these typical situations, insurers file rates that reflect a provision for profit and contingencies that is a percentage of premium. The percentage of premium is justified using data about the percentage that is charged in other states and for comparable risks in other industries. The notable exceptions are personal lines (automobile and homeowners, which are widely regulated) and the state of California (which regulates many commercial insurance products using a return-on-nominal-equity approach).

In the typical case, the provision for profit and contingencies is not computed using a return-on-equity approach. This does **not** mean that the profit provision is set without reference to the capital markets. Bingham (Chapter 4) says no body of comparative reference data exists for return-on-premium as a function of risk. In fact, insurers have available to them the return-on-premium data for hundreds of insurance companies in dozens of states in which insurance profit provisions are not regulated. This return-on-premium data is the appropriate basis for determining profit provisions when it is inappropriate to develop a full analysis of payment patterns and their probabilities.

Even in California, the Department of Insurance has adopted rules for the calculation of the rate of return that substitute nominal surplus for the company's actual surplus. The effect is that provisions for profits are set as percentages of premiums, much as Mintel (Chapter 9) describes.

Anecdotal information this writer has accumulated over the years suggests that actuaries have used measures of standard deviation and measures of the probability of ruin when using statistical methods to price risk. In either approach, the actuary tries to select a parameter that generates an appropriate risk charge as a percentage of premium. The probability-of-ruin benchmark is often equivalent in practice to a standard deviation benchmark because the actual results must depart from expected by a certain number of standard deviations to trigger the event of ruin. If the methods described here were widely used in rate filings, the effect would be that capital costs on property-casualty insurance vary roughly in proportion to the standard deviation of results for a wide range of insurance products. The charge per standard deviation would vary from product to product.

Bingham (Chapter Four) suggests the use of "operating return" instead of return on premium. This seems to be the same as return-on-premium in practice because each line will have a single ratio of operating return to premium. Bingham seems to be conceding that the company's capital structure is not *necessarily* relevant to the decision about the provision for profit. Given that one will use a method that is independent of the capital structure of the firm, the use of operating return presents at least one small challenge that does not appear when using return-on-premium directly. Operating returns are analogous to returns on assets, but in the case of very short-tail lines of insurance with high levels of risk the operating return will be quite high and quite unlike the returns on assets generated by typical investments. For example, a return-on-premium of 30% might be appropriate for property catastrophe insurance. If the duration of liabilities were 0.2 years, this would be an operating return (as defined by Bingham) of 150%. It is difficult to see how this result can be obtained by analogy with investments, no matter how correct it is. Arguing by analogy with investment returns has not worked in practice for many companies in many lines of insurance.

CRITICISM OF IRR MODELS, INCLUDING CAPM

Given the axioms listed in Table 1, internal-rate-of-return (IRR) rules are inappropriate for insurance. Yet IRR rules have served the investment community well for more than a century. It is not surprising, then, that return-on-investment rules are good approximations to the formulas above when the decision is characterized by cash flows that are outward at first, and inward later, with the uncertainty about the inward cash flows increasing over time (at a decreasing rate). All of the internal-rate-of-return (IRR) rules discussed in investment literature are special cases of the formulas shown above. Therefore IRR rules generally work well in pricing bonds. This derivation is shown in Appendix 2.

The cost of risk is always a cost. The major problem with the ratemaking methods that impute IRR is that they get the minus sign wrong. IRR methods discount losses more as the losses' riskiness increases. This isn't just counterintuitive, it is wrong. No one really thinks that riskier loss payments should be discounted more than predictable loss payments. Even D'Arcy and Bingham imply that something must be done to make their equations practical when comparing lines of equal duration and different risk.

IRR methods ask for an explicit allocation of surplus to the risks in each rate filing. As McClenahan points out in Chapter 8, "...no matter how much the rate-of-return advocate may wish to ignore the fact, there is no such thing as North Dakota Private Passenger Automobile Surplus - unless, of course, we are dealing with a company which writes North Dakota private passenger automobile insurance exclusively." There is, however, a probability distribution of outcomes for North Dakota Private Passenger Automobile which determines the average number of units of risk per car-year, and there is a cost per unit of risk in the capital markets as shown in Figure 2.

Applying approaches based on the Capital Asset Pricing Model (CAPM), even to generalized problems of asset management, is not always appropriate. CAPM has been criticized for its lack of predictive power and its restrictive assumptions. Indeed, one assumption of the Capital Asset Pricing Model is that the decision-maker is trying to optimize the performance of an infinitely divisible portfolio of equity investments. This assumption alone should cause one to wonder why CAPM should inform us about the cost of capital for insurance. Finally, ROLL and ROSS (1994) have shown that in general it is not practical to calculate the parameters of the Capital Asset Pricing Model from data about portfolios of securities.

CAPM is inconsistent with Efficient Market Principle because it values risk in proportion to the variance of returns. The mean and variance of a set of uncertain outcomes are sufficient to determine the cost of risk under the axioms in Table 1 only if the possible outcomes are normally distributed. This is rarely the case in practical situations, even for portfolio management. The widely used Black-Scholes model, for example, assumes that the logarithms of market values are normally distributed, which implies distribution of returns much more skewed than a normal distribution. In practical problems, variance loads lose a lot of information about the risks of adverse results. This criticism applies to other approaches that rely on one statistic of the probability distribution of outcomes, including those based on probability of ruin, e.g., Pierson (Chapter 5) and Kreps (Chapter 6).

Finally, one does not need the Capital Asset Pricing Model, with its elegant use of the property of the variance of a probability distribution, to get to the common-sense idea that risks whose outcomes vary with the direction of outcomes of the broad capital markets will command a higher risk premium than those that do not. Figure 3 shows one way to estimate the cost of capital for an investment or an insurance business in light of how its outcomes correspond to some composite market index.

SUMMARY

There are many implications for those who make decisions about insurance, whether as underwriters, actuaries, marketers, investors, or regulators.

There is a cost of risk for insurance companies when they underwrite a set of insurance contracts. That cost of risk is a function of the probabilities of gains and losses, with the possible gains and losses expressed at their present value. A fundamental economic analysis shows that the cost of risk is constant per unit of exposure. The number of units of risk per unit of exposure depends on the nature of the exposure that is being rated.

The "Modern Theory of Finance" is irrelevant for rate filings. Internal rate-of-return calculations play no role because the assumptions underlying such methods are not valid for insurance. Per unit of risk, the cost of risk is the same in insurance and in investments.

In most practical ratemaking situations, equations for the computation of the cost of risk can be applied to compute the cost of risk per unit of exposure. The equations rely on the same forecasts of loss payments under a range of scenarios that underlie the estimate of the average loss cost per unit of exposure. The cost of risk is found from the solution of the following three simultaneous equations, where the parameter s is found in the capital markets:

$$\pi = E[x] - P[x]$$

$$E[x] = \sum_k \sum_j \sum_i p(k)\, p\left(x = x_i \middle| t = t_j, k\right) x_i v_{t_j}$$

$$P[x] = -\frac{\pi}{s} \ln \sum_k p(k) \exp\left[-\frac{s}{\pi} \sum_j -\frac{\pi}{s} \ln \sum_i p\left(x = x_i \middle| t = t_j, k\right) e^{-s\frac{x_i v_{t_j}}{\pi}} \right]$$

The cost of a unit of risk can be observed in the capital markets just as the cost of bread can be observed in the markets in which bread is exchanged. It is embodied in a parameter, s. This parameter can be estimated using the equations and data about the prices at which transactions are actually priced.

Loss payments that will be paid some time after the premium is collected should be adjusted to their present value at the time the premium is collected using the **risk-free** rate of return, not some higher rate of return. The risk-free discount factor is the factor that converts currency that will be received with certainty at some future time into its value today. It can be read from the newspaper each day (and from the Internet even on weekends). Discounting at a higher rate of return, such as a company's internal profit target (return on equity), leads to an understatement of the economic cost of the losses.

Loss forecasts are uncertain. The greater the uncertainty, the greater the cost of capital, and the higher the indicated premium rate.

When data is insufficient to do the calculations explicitly, or when the desired accuracy does not merit a large amount of study, an informed estimate considering the cost of capital for other lines of insurance will be more appropriate than an informed estimate considering the yield rates on investments. Internal-rate-of-return formulas that underlie the calculations of yield rates do not apply to insurance because they rely on the **assumption** that cash flows are outward first and inward later. This assumption applies to investments, but not to insurance.

Because the capital markets are vastly larger than any one risk, the cost of risk is directly proportional to the size of the risk. If the cost of risk in underwriting \$20 million of auto insurance is \$1 million, the cost of risk in underwriting \$40 million of auto insurance is \$2 million. This means that the **cost of risk is a percentage of the premium**

underwritten, and the percentage varies from one kind of insurance to the next depending on the riskiness of the kind of insurance. (Precisely the same statements can be said about the markets for commodities, or common stocks, or any other type of risk.)

To a specific company, the cost of risk depends on all of the company's assets and liabilities. Unless regulators interfere with the capital markets, the company's other assets and liabilities and the capital markets' cost for one unit of risk will affect the company's willingness to extend its underwriting leverage in a way that optimizes the competitiveness of the insurance markets.

After a careful analysis, there is no reason to adopt methods based on internal-rate-of-return calculations. A careful exposition of the problem, using a minimal set of assumptions in the tradition of Arrow and Debreu, leads to the same simple conclusions that McClenahan, Mintel, and Toney have suggested for other reasons.

BIBLIOGRAPHY

1. Karl Borch (1962), "Equilibrium in a Reinsurance Market", Econometrica 30, p. 424-444.

2. J. David Cummins and Scott A. Harrington (1987), Fair Rate of Return in Property-Liability Insurance, Kluwer-Nijhoff Publishing, Boston.

3. Gerard Debreu (1959), Theory of Value: An Axiomatic Analysis of Economic Equilibrium, Cowles Foundation for Research in Economics, Yale University Press, 1959.

4. Hans U. Gerber (1979), An Introduction to Mathematical Risk Theory, Huebner Foundation Monograph 8, Wharton School of the University of Pennsylvania, Richard D. Irwin Inc.

5. G. F. Michelbacher and Nestor R. Roos (1970), Multiple-Line Insurers: Their Nature and Operation, McGraw-Hill

6. Judith K. Mintel (1983), Insurance Rate Litigation, Kluwer-Nijhoff Publishing, Boston.

7. Richard Roll and Stephen A. Ross (1994), "On the Cross-Sectional Relation between Expected Returns and Betas," Journal of Finance, Vol. 49, No. 1, p. 101.

8. Stephen A. Ross (1976), "The Arbitrage Theory of Capital Asset Pricing", Journal of Economic Theory, Vol. 13, p 341-360.

9. Stephen A. Ross (1994), "Survivorship in Finance", Record of the Society of Actuaries, Vol. 20, No. 1, p.1.

10. Giuseppe Russo and Oakley E. Van Slyke (1996), "Interpreting Model Output: The California Earthquake Authority and the Cost of Capital of the Reinsurance Layer," Call Papers of the Special Interest Seminar on Dynamic Financial Modeling, Casualty Actuarial Society Forum, July 1996.

11. James Stone, 1973a, "A Theory of Capacity and the Insurance of Catastrophic Risks, Part I", Journal of Risk and Insurance, June 1973.

12. James Stone, 1973b, "A Theory of Capacity and the Insurance of Catastrophic Risks, Part II", Journal of Risk and Insurance, June and September, 1973.

13. Oakley E. Van Slyke (1995), "A General Theory of Finance", Proceedings of the 5th AFIR Colloquium, September, 1995, vol. II, p. 585.

APPENDIX 1

THE AXIOMATIC DEVELOPMENT

This appendix sets out the axiomatic development of Equation **1**. It provides an overview only, as the references include much important material and the mathematical development is rather difficult to read.

Debreu (1959), in the classic Theory of Value: An Axiomatic Analysis of Economic Equilibrium, shows that an equilibrium structure exists for the economy. In this equilibrium, the prices and amounts of all goods and instruments of production are such that they maximize the value of the economy.

A general outline of the argument is shown in Figure 1.1 on the following page.

This conclusion rests on the following theorem, which Debreu proves in one of the most demanding proofs in economics. Debreu states the theorem in careful mathematical statements which I am merely paraphrasing here.

> If a decision-maker can choose between any pair of alternatives offered, and if the choices of the decision-maker are consistent, then the decision-maker will make choices as if he or she had assigned numerical values to the alternatives and selected the alternative with the highest numerical value.

By consistent, Debreu means that if the decision-maker prefers A over B and prefers B over C, the decision-maker will prefer A over C. Also, if the decision-maker is indifferent between A and B and between B and C, he or she will be indifferent between A and C.

BORCH (1962) extended this to show that in a simple economy consisting only of the reinsurance of a particular policy, with the alternatives limited to various shares of the total to be reinsured, the economic players would share in the reinsurance risk in proportion to a unique parameter of each. Each player would take a share of the risk. Each player would get that same share of the reward, here called π. However measured, the ratio of π to risk undertaken would be the same for all the players.

FIGURE 1.1. SUPPLY AND DEMAND

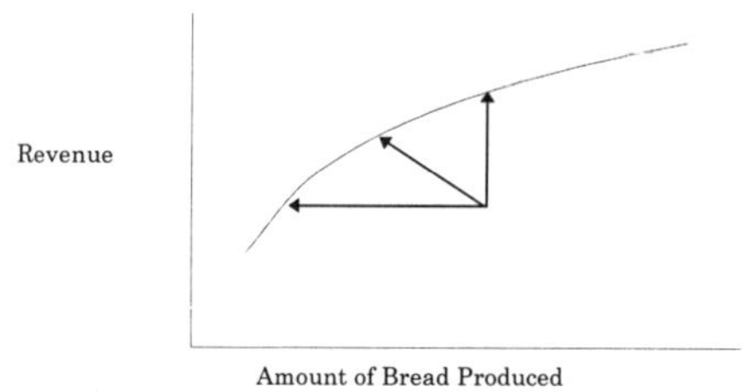

1A. PARETO-OPTIMAL FRONTIER. Each baker of bread will seek to bake the least possible number of loaves for a given reward, or seek to get the greatest total price for a given number of loaves. There is a limit, or frontier, to the amount that can be charged, however. The limit is defined by the *demand* for bread.

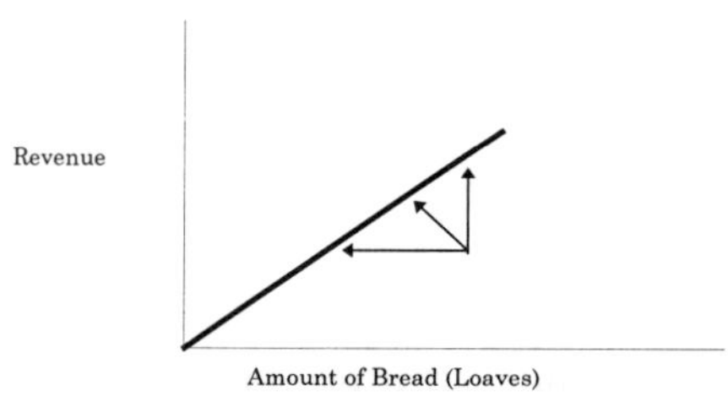

1B. CONSTANT PRICE PER UNIT. Each baker will receive a certain price per loaf of bread. No one baker can affect the market's price per loaf. No baker can charge more than the market price. The efficient market principle states that the price is as if each baker and each consumer uses all of the available information about the bread.

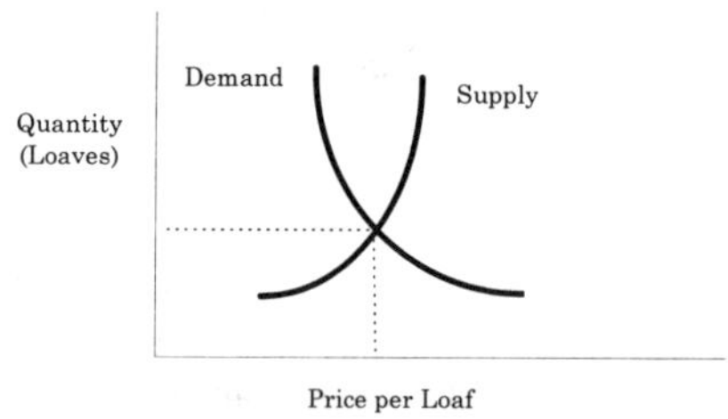

1C. EQUILIBRIUM OF SUPPLY AND DEMAND. For the economy as a whole, as the price of bread increases, the demand decreases. As the price increases, the supply increases. The demand schedule is related to the frontier in Fig. 1A. Prices move toward the equilibrium level even though every individual strives to be at its own point on the Pareto-optimum frontier.

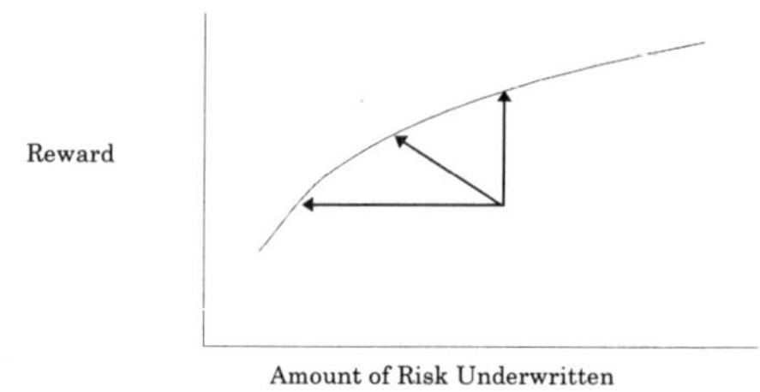

2A. PARETO-OPTIMAL FRONTIER FOR RI Each firm will seek to take the least possible risk fo given reward or to get the greatest possible reward fo given level of risk. Borch (1962) showed the equati for Pareto-optimal behavior which are consistent with efficient market principle.

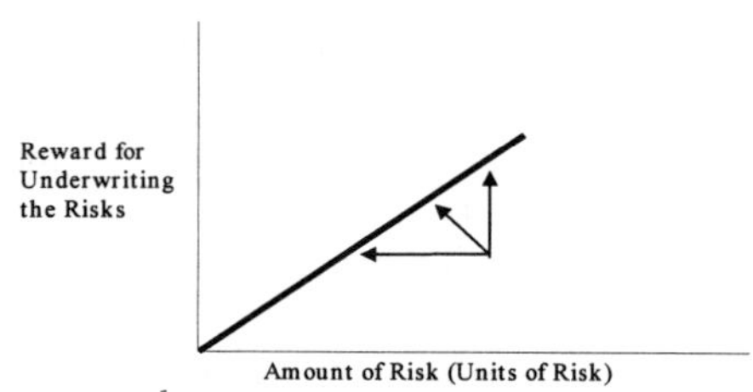

2B. CONSTANT PRICE PER UNIT OF RISK. V Slyke (1995) extended Borch's work, showing tha implies that each investor or underwriter is paid a mar price per unit of risk. We assume no one investor underwriter can affect the capital market's price per u of risk.

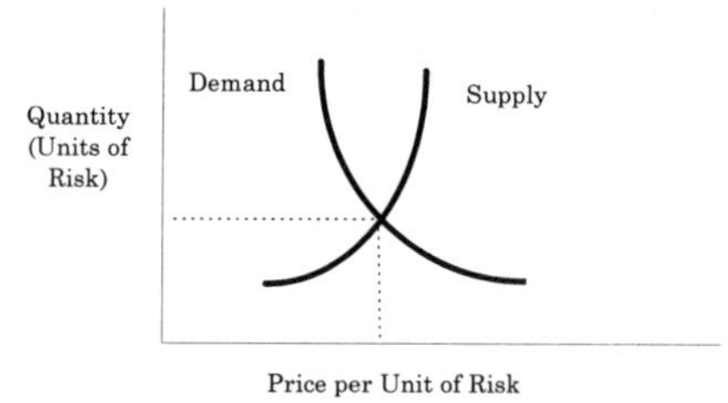

2C. EQUILIBRIUM OF SUPPLY AND DEMA FOR RISKY TRANSACTIONS. Capital plays m roles. For the economy as a whole, the equilibrium pr for capital in its role in underwriting risk in on the sup schedule from the equations shown above. Regardless the demand schedule, these equations hold equilibrium.

Gerber (1979) shows the train of thought in a very readable way. At page 70, he lists five properties that a principle of premium calculation should have. These are:

1. Non-negative safety loading
2. No rip-off
3. Consistency
4. Additivity
5. Iterativity

He then supplements these (p. 73) with prohibitions against charging nothing for the cost of risk and against charging the full value of the loss for a chance of a loss (with the chance less than 100%). Gerber shows that only an exponential charge for risk such as that in Borch's result is consistent with these axioms.

Borch and Gerber considered the static case: risk exists at the time of the choice, and is resolved immediately upon the completion of the transaction. They ignored the time value of money. VAN SLYKE (1995) extended this work to include the time value of money. The result is a clear distinction between the effect of currency prices and the effect of risk aversion.

To see that such a distinction is reasonable, consider two risks with very different payment patterns, property catastrophe cover and an investment in bonds. The losses under property catastrophe cover are realized at roughly the time the premium is received. This is the timing considered by Borch and Gerber. They showed that the cost of capital is in proportion to the share of the risk that is reinsured. This means that if a benchmark risk is established, every part of every treaty would involve a certain number of units of risk, and every unit of risk would command the same cost.

Bonds, on the other hand, involve payments over many years. Most of the risk arises from the possibility of default on all or part of the principle. Consider a set of bonds with a range of different chances of default. As the chance of default decreases, the price of the bond approaches that of a bond issued by the Federal government. The yield on such bonds is called the risk-free rate of interest. That is, in the limit, as the risk of default approaches zero, the discount factor for the bond's cash flows approaches the risk-free rate of return. Therefore, the risk-free rate of return must appear in the equations of the value of investments and insurance risks, and appear at the limit.

There are three levels of summation in the equations above. Note that a series of payments that are *certain* to be paid or received over time are precisely as valuable in the capital markets as the sum of their present values. Therefore, amounts that are to be combined across time using risk-free present-value factors must be expressed as the value they would have if they were certain to occur, which is their economic value. Therefore, when adding amounts over time, if there is uncertainty in the outcomes at a certain time for a certain scenario, the economic value of the possible outcomes must be found by application of the exponential adjustments indicated by Borch. Only these economic values can be offset against one another over time; to do otherwise is to combine apples and oranges. This is the reason for the innermost summation. Finally, the present values, or economic values, of all of the possible outcomes under the various scenarios entail a risk because of the uncertainty about which scenario will be realized. The cost of capital for that risk must be recognized by an exponential adjustment as indicated by Borch. This is the reason for the outermost summation.

The Efficient Market Principle states that in the aggregate, prices reflect all of the information available to all of the players. The exponential charge for risk in the equations above preserves all of the information in the probability distribution of outcomes. The use of prices for risk-free Treasury securities preserves all of the information about the time value of money. The Efficient Market Principal implies that the price of capital will be the same in all capital markets. That is, there will be a unique value of s that reflects the capital markets as a whole. Just as the price of bread varies from one transaction to the next depending on differences in shipping, spoilage, and so on, the price of capital will vary from transaction to transaction. But in the aggregate, just as the price of bread is set by the markets for bread, other commodities, and factors of production, so is the price of capital set by the capital markets.

And this is why the cost of risk per unit of risk is the same for industrial bonds and the $2 billion excess of $4 billion layer of the California Earthquake Authority, as shown in Figure 2 above.

APPENDIX 2

IRR RULES ARE A SPECIAL CASE OF EQUATION 1

Assuming there is a single scenario, the economic value of an investment is

$$P[x] = -\frac{\pi}{s}\ln E\left[\exp\left(-s\frac{x}{\pi}\right)\right] \tag{2.1}$$

where x is the present value of a cash flow that has a certain probability of occurring and the expectation operator E is the probability-weighted average. The present value of a cash flow is the amount of money required today to purchase a risk-free instrument with the same cash flow.

$$x_i = \sum_{t=0}^{\infty} v(t)x_i(t) \tag{2.2}$$

Consider the following investment:

- A single scenario.
- An investment of I at time $t=0$.
- Cash flows at later times are expected to be inward. (More precisely, all $\mu(t)>0,\ t>0$, where $\mu(t)$ is the expected value of $x(t)$.)
- A constant risk-free rate of return, that is,

  $$v(t) = v^t = \left(1+R_f\right)^{-t}$$

- A risk premium proportional to the variance of the possible cash flows, assumed to be because the possible cash flows are normally distributed. Using **2.1**, the constant of proportionality is found to be $2\pi/s$. Then at time t

  $$P[x|t] = \mu(t) - s\frac{\sigma^2(t)}{2\pi}$$

- The variance of the cash flows at any point in time is perceived to vary with the expected cash flow, and the ratio of the variance to the expected cash flow at any point in time is expected to increase over time (perhaps because it seems harder to forecast far into the future). That is,

$$\sigma^2(t) = c_1\mu(t)\left(1 - c_2^t\right) \qquad c_1 > 0 \quad 0 < c_2 < 1 \tag{2.3}$$

The decision rule suggests the transaction should be accepted whenever the risk-adjusted present value of the uncertain cash flows is greater than the investment *I*. That is,

$$\sum_{t=0}^{\infty} v(t)P\left[x|t\right] > I \tag{2.4}$$

Substituting the specific values for this example:

$$\sum_{t=0}^{\infty}\left(1 + R_f\right)^{-t}\left(\mu(t) - \left(s\frac{\sigma^2(t)}{2\pi}\right)\right) > I \tag{2.5}$$

and

$$\sum_{t=0}^{\infty}\left(1 + R_f\right)^{-t}\left(\mu(t)\left(1 - s\frac{c_1}{2\pi}\left(1 - c_2^t\right)\right)\right) > I \tag{2.6}$$

If $c_1 = 2\frac{\pi}{s}$, then

$$\sum_{t=0}^{\infty}\left(1 + R_f\right)^{-t}\mu(t)c_2^t > I \tag{2.7}$$

Define a variable *IRR* such that

$$c_2 = \frac{1 + R_f}{1 + IRR} \tag{2.8}$$

Then

$$\sum_{t=0}^{\infty}(1 + IRR)^{-t}\mu(t) > I \tag{2.9}$$

That is, the decision-maker considering the hypothetical investment should adopt an *IRR* decision rule, and the minimum *IRR* is found from

$$\frac{\sigma^2(t)}{\mu(t)} = \left(\frac{2\pi}{s}\right)\left[1 - \left(\frac{1+R_f}{1+IRR}\right)^t\right] \tag{2.10}$$

or

$$(1+IRR)^t > \frac{\left(1+R_f\right)^t}{\left(1 - s\dfrac{\sigma^2(t)}{2\pi\mu(t)}\right)} \tag{2.11}$$

In this expression, the construction of the hypothetical investment is such that the value of *IRR* is the same for all points in time. The assumption is that the variance at each time *t* increases with the mean of the expected return at time *t* and the ratio of variance to mean increases with time asymptotically toward a maximum that is a function of the expected financial gain and the market's aversion toward risk. Recall that the cost of risk, π, is the difference between the present value of expected returns at the risk-free rate of interest and the present value at the rate *IRR* (which is the maximum one should pay for the investment).

Figure 2.1 shows the curve for the anticipated variance of future inward cash flows that is consistent with the IRR decision rule under the assumptions of this example. The value of *IRR* determines how quickly the curve rises towards its limit.

FIGURE 2.1

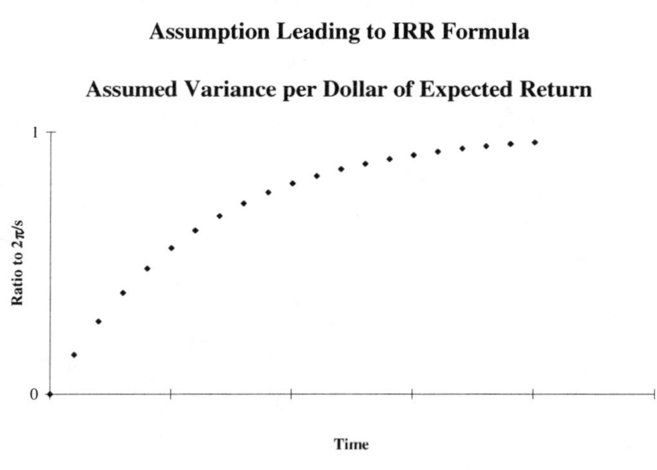

This set of assumptions is not as restrictive as it seems. Investments in bonds and capital equipment are characterized by an increase in risk over time, but not without limit. Also, in such investments, most of the risk in dollar terms is concentrated at the time the investment matures. Changes to the assumed level of risk at early periods will have only a small effect on the computed value of *IRR*. It is therefore not surprising that IRR rules work well for investments in bonds and many kinds of capital equipment.

The Discounted Cash Flow Approach

Stephen P. D'Arcy

Insurance Profitability

Charles L. McClenahan

Review by Robert P. Eramo

The authors provide an excellent presentation of their respective views. Their debate clearly is between viewing return on surplus or return on premium as the most appropriate measure of return. This is a debate of importance to more than the insurance industry. Utilities in this country have been subjected to rate regulation for years, and the decision to approve utility rates is frequently based on factors similar to those in the authors' papers. When surplus and premium are substituted with equity and sales, respectively, one clearly sees the application to other industries.

It is important to realize that most businesses experience periods in their history when market conditions permit unusually high rates of return. These conditions may result from the newness of a product or internal efficiencies permitting a high rate of return. In a free market, high rates of return can be a key factor motivating the promotion and development of new products and services. Governments and government regulators should do little to discourage rapid development induced by high rates of return.

It is probably not the authors' intent to provide regulators ammunition that stifles innovation and progress. Unfortunately, these papers may be read by populists seeking political gain. Resulting pricing constraints, strictly driven by the factors covered by these papers, can stifle innovation and progress. The retardation of progress in the long run hurts all of us.

Specifically, in the property and casualty insurance industry, certain insurance companies have presented in certain periods of their history their stockholders with extraordinarily high rates of return. These high rates of return can be justified in most instances. The movement to direct sale of personal lines insurance is one example. If rigid regulation had been applied to companies making the move to direct sales, all consumers would have suffered paying insurance rates higher than necessary. Other property and casualty companies have innovated in the commercial lines, benefiting from the minimal rate regulation prevalent in the commercial lines. The massive movement to self insurance has been facilitated by a revolution in fronting arrangements spear-headed by certain property and casualty companies. Both business and consumers benefit with the ability to buy risk management services from a number of third party administrators. The risk management program is specifically designed, and prices are negotiated at a number of levels by the insurer.

In conclusion, both authors provide fine studies on the rate-of-return question. But one must never suggest that factors treated in these papers become the sole determinant of an appropriate price. In business, those who innovate must be rewarded. And the value of the innovation is frequently not easily quantifiable and reflected in some ratemaking formula. If a regulator limits his decision making to known historical factors in his approval procedures, in the long run, all will suffer paying higher prices and receiving services less than what technology permits.

Government regulators must recognize the need for high rates of return at critical points of economic development. Most importantly, regulators must realize that over time innovations are copied, eventually causing both prices and rates of return to fall to more normal levels. The regulator best meets his goal of reducing excess profits by encouraging competition, not by brow beating innovators. Regulation that caters to "price controls" makes everyone lose. It will be tragic if these fine papers serve as fodder for regulation that stifles innovation and that limits the workings of a free market.

The Discounted Cash Flow Approach

Stephen P. D'Arcy

Insurance Profitability

Charles L. McClenahan

Review by Mark W. Littman

As mathematicians move from the halls of academia to become professional actuaries in the insurance industry, it becomes quickly apparent that neither carefully crafted textbook problems nor right answers exist. In the case of appropriate standards for property casualty insurance profit margins, I would suggest that the lack of a single answer is directly dependent on the lack of a single definition of the problem.

As McClenahan succinctly described in the opening paragraph of his paper, it is "in the eye of the beholder." Persons seeking an unconditioned, authoritative response to the question, "How much profit should an insurance company earn?" can only be disappointed when the response begins with, "It depends…."

I turn my remarks now to specific comments on the approaches advocated by the authors.

DISCOUNTED CASH FLOW

In his advocacy of the discounted cash flow approach, D'Arcy suggests that an insurer (investor) would not write a policy (invest in the business) if the underwriting profit margin were below the level at which the net present value of the policy cash flow were zero. To challenge this statement would be to challenge "motherhood and apple pie." In fact, I concur with virtually all of D'Arcy's remarks. I would like only to spell out a few underlying assumptions and identify two considerations.

The approach would appear to suggest an underwriting decision horizon of one year or less. It would also implicitly assume that a company is free to write or not to write (including to non-renew) policies for a particular coverage, line of insurance, or geographic area. Among the many considerations that should be made in evaluating the "to-commit or not-to-commit" decision are these two:

- Marginal versus average expenses

    Microeconomics makes an important distinction between marginal and average costs in the context of the business owner's decision to continue operating, even in the face of a lack of profits. To the extent that variable costs are being covered and fixed costs only partially covered, it may still be prudent for the business to be continued.

- Scope of business decision

  D'Arcy appears silent on the definition of the "insurance policy" upon which an investment decision is being made. I would suggest that it will probably encompass:

  - more than one product line, considering the total account sales orientation of most companies, and

  - more than one year, considering the fortuitous nature of one year's results and the longer-term focus of insurance decision making.

RETURN ON SALES APPROACH

McClenahan presents a thoughtful discussion of the relative strengths and weaknesses of evaluating a profit margin in the context of rate-of-return regulation. In his conclusion, he advocates a return-on-sales approach, where results would be independent of the relationship between premium and equity.

McClenahan says, "It can be as simple as the 1921 NAIC Profit Formula which allowed 5% of premium for underwriting profit (and an additional 3% for conflagrations) or it can be as complicated as the use of benchmark writings-to-surplus ratios applied to permitted return-on-equity provisions." These, however, do not appear very satisfactory in terms of generating unanimous support. The results from the first way would be fully dependent on the "beholder," and those from the second would be subject to the pitfalls of asking the questions, "How much surplus?" and "What rate of return?"

In my opinion, the most striking concept that McClenahan raises is a reminder that, "it is the *rates* which are being regulated, not the rates-of-return." It appears that, in practice, rate regulation has become rate-of-return regulation (which asks unsolvable questions). And, as noted above, even the substitution of sales for equity in the formula does not eliminate the difficult issues.

Rather than asking, "What is an appropriate profit margin for rates?," I would suggest asking a different question, "How do we know if the market is competitive?" McClenahan, in fact, raises this alternate view on the profit issue in his Profitability Standards section: "The proper benchmark for excessiveness for a regulator is that which will produce the desired market characteristics."

What are the desired market characteristics? A short list of desirable and measurable attributes would include:

- a large number of companies competing
- a small proportion of the market insured through involuntary market mechanisms
- a small concentration of market shares of leading companies
- a reasonable number of new companies
- a reasonably small number of retiring companies.

If these characteristics sound like those of the textbook world of perfect competition (even without perfect information), so be it. If ever in the "real world" such a market could exist, the property casualty insurance market would be a likely place.

In such a competitive market, self-interest and greed will tend to force the entire market to the so-called equilibrium "right" price. These same forces will encourage product innovation, improved customer service, and other desirable behaviors. The efficient companies will thrive and the inefficient companies will struggle and perhaps not survive. The "right" answer for the profit margin in rates will emerge by itself, unassisted by the hand of regulation.

What would be left for the rate regulator to do? Resources could be directed toward assisting in gathering and publishing competitive rating information, evaluating the competitiveness of the market, and guiding corrective action as necessary. Could "less" really be "more"?

CONCLUDING REMARKS

There is no single right answer to the profit question. All of the various stakeholders must decide for themselves. I applaud D'Arcy and McClenahan for their contributions, presenting views on the subject from the perspectives of an investor and a rate regulator.

The academic discussion of the "right answer" has gone on for a long time and will probably continue. I would suggest that McClenahan's remarks regarding the relationship between rate excessiveness (and inadequacy) and the desired market characteristics is a relatively new vein of research that should be further explored for practical application.